Marutas of Unit 731

*Human Experimentation of the
Forgotten Asian Auschwitz*

Pacific Atrocities Education

Marutas of Unit 731

Human Experimentation of the Forgotten Asian Auschwitz

JENNY CHAN

Marutas of Unit 731

Human Experimentation of the Forgotten Asian Auschwitz

Written by
Jenny Chan

Editor
Barbara Halperin

Published by Pacific Atrocities Education

All rights reserved. Printed in the United States of America. No part of this book may be reproduced in any manner whatsoever without written permission except in the case of brief quotations embodied in critical articles and reviews. For information, address Pacific Atrocities Education, 730 Commercial Street, San Francisco, CA 94108.

Paperback ISBN: 978-1-947766-32-7

E-book ISBN: 978-1-947766-16-7

Table of Contents

Introduction _____ 1

Chapter 1. US-Asia Relationship _____ 7

Chapter 2. The Beginning of an Evil Genius _____ 15

Chapter 3. A Beta Testing Site _____ 21

Chapter 4. Establishing Pingfan _____ 31

Chapter 5. Experiences at the Human Experimentation Complex _____ 47

Chapter 6. Vivisection _____ 63

Chapter 7. Anta Testing Grounds _____ 81

Chapter 8. Overall Advance from the Laboratory Creations _____ 111

Chapter 9. The End of the War _____ 117

Introduction

Unit 731 was a secret biological and chemical warfare research complex created and developed by the Imperial Japanese Army. Although it provided research opportunities for the brightest Japanese scientists in WWII, thousands of people died as victims of gruesome experiments performed ostensibly in the name of science. At the height of the research facility, no employee of Unit 731 foresaw its demise.

As Emperor Hirohito signed the surrender agreement, documenting the end of the Japanese Empire, an order was issued to leave no survivors and every captive was killed. By the time the Soviets arrived in Manchuria, they found a destroyed facility with animals in cages, human remains, and most of the staff already evacuated.

Under the supervision of Ishii Shiro, Unit 731 and its subsidiaries not only regularly conducted vivisection on humans, they were also proud of the weaponry produced as a result. Initial appalling experiments at the Anta testing ground included testing the effectiveness of various bombs used on victims tied to stakes, exposure to extreme cold to document the effect of frostbite on victims' limbs, and exposure to severe changes in air pressure to test human limits for the purpose of airplane development. These were only a few of many experiments conducted in the decade in which the unit was active.

When scientists needed more victims for human experimentation, they simply had to fill out a request and, the majority of the time, the Kwantung Army would make a special human delivery. The bound victims' heads were covered with sacks as they were transported on trains and then in vehicles through underground tunnels to the gate of Unit 731 where experiments would commence. Otherwise known as "maruta", which means logs in Japanese, Unit 731 were not thought of as humans but merely as test subjects. Once exhausted by the experiments, marutas were viewed as unusable material and subsequently killed. As stated by Mitomo Kazuo during the Khabarovsk Trial, "At the beginning of September 1944, two Russians were shot dead in my presence by a gendarme at the cattle cemetery and were buried there. This was done on the orders of Lieutenant Nakajima. They were shot because no more experiments could be performed on them in view of their exhausted state and unsuitability for further experimentation." This kind of brutality in Unit 731 and that of its subsidiaries was not an isolated incident for the Imperial Japanese Army during WWII.

My grandmother had always told me about their survival stories during WWII. She told me about the executions that regularly were carried out in King's Park in Hong Kong during the Japanese occupation. Under threat of severe punishment, families were forced to trade all their wealth for military yen. Like most women at the time, my grandmother avoided being outside and darkened her face with charcoal to prevent being raped by Japanese soldiers. However, having been educated in the United States, I had not learned in school about the Pacific Asia War brutality and had ignored most of what my grandma told me until I read the book *Rape of Nanking*.

Regretting not listening to my grandmother, my friend and I co-founded Pacific Atrocities Education with the purpose of visiting the forgotten past of the WWII Pacific Theater. Curiosity led me to visit comfort women in Shanxi in Northern China in 2014 which then led to my writing the historical fiction, *The Undrowning Lotus*. In 2015, I attended a conference about the Pacific Asia War hosted by the Global Alliance. Wang Xuan spoke about villagers with rotten legs who were victims of biological warfare waged by the Imperial Japanese Army. It was there when I first learned about Unit 731. The biological weapons victims were unable even to put socks on their legs which never healed from glanders and anthrax left on Chinese soil during WWII. Seventy years after the war, through Wang Xuan's relentless efforts, a means of curing rotten legs finally was found. To learn more about Wang Xuan and her work, check out *Seeking Justice for Biological Warfare Victims of Unit 731*.

After years of researching Unit 731, I was appalled by the fact that most of the scientists who worked there suffered no consequences nor faced any criminal justice charges due to immunity granted to them by the United States government. Since the U.S. scientists were unable to conduct the same types of human experiments, they were more than eager when the Japanese scientists offered them their real-world experience in exchange for their freedom. For the reader's enjoyment, I did not insert any pictures of human experimentation in this book, but readers can check this link:

https://www.pacificatrocities.org/human-experimentation.html.

Chapter 1

US-Asia Relationship

U.S. intervention in Japan began in 1851 when Matthew Perry arrived in Japanese waters with a squadron of Navy ships authorized by President Millard Fillmore. Japan had been an isolated country and had captured many U.S. sailors in its waters. Perry's mission was two-fold—to rescue the sailors who were destined for imprisonment or death in Japan and to open up Japan for trade.

Since Japan had been isolated for centuries, the West was far more militarily advanced and in the area of weaponry. With Matthew Perry's gunboat diplomacy, a steamboat in Japanese waters bearing gifts for the emperor helped convince the Japanese of the West's superiority. The Japanese accepted an agreement to release the U.S. sailors as well as open a port for refueling.[1]

---

[1] "The United States and the Opening to Japan, 1853." *U.S. Department of State*, U.S. Department of State, history.state.gov/milestones/1830-1860/opening-to-japan.

During that time period, many Americans believed in Manifest Destiny, meaning that they were destined by God to rule the North American continent as well as God's wish to rule the world. While the Qing Dynasty of China failed to catch up to the modern world, missionaries were rushing to Guangdong, China to fruitlessly convert Chinese into Christians. Merchants were also busily trading opium for Chinese tea and silk. By the mid-1800s, China was carved up like a melon by the militarily superior Western Powers.[2]

Japan saw what had happened to China as a result of its inability to advance in technology, combined with Matthew Perry's demand for the Treaty of Kanagawa on March 31, 1854, which opened two Japanese ports, Shimoda and Hakodate. The treaty also granted the U.S. rights, thus leading to the start of Japan's era of industrialization during which Japan quickly learned about and adapted western ways.

Kaneko Kentaro was born a year after Matthew Perry's first arrival in Japanese waters and became one of the most influential politicians in Japan's modern history. Born into a samurai family of the

---

[2] "1750-1919: China and the West: Imperialism, Opium, and Self-Strengthening (1800-1921): Central Themes and Key Points: Asia for Educators: Columbia University." *1750-1919: China and the West: Imperialism, Opium, and Self-Strengthening (1800-1921) | Central Themes and Key Points | Asia for Educators | Columbia University*, afe.easia.columbia.edu/main_pop/kpct/kp_imperialism.htm.

Fukuoka Clan, the Japan that Kaneko's birth was very different from that of his parents' era, the Tokugawa era where shoguns were considered the most powerful class and Japan was under feudalism. Matthew Perry's arrival had shown the people the Tokugawa's policy's weakness and, given the famine at the time, led to an uprising of the peasant class.

By the time Kaneko was a teenager, two powerful clans, Choshu and Satsuma combined forces to topple the Tokugawa's power structure and the Meiji Restoration era began. In that new era, Japan ended its feudalistic rule, brought about social, political, and economic changes, and opened up to Western trade and influence in order to build up its technology for stronger military power. It was the quickest modernization any East Asian country had ever seen in that time period.[3]

Japan had sent many of its young minds to the west. From 1871 to 1873, the best mission was the Iwakura Embassy comprised of 48 scholars and administrators, including Kaneko. They toured the U.S., the United Kingdom, France, and Germany. As a result, Kaneko studied at Harvard University.[4] Fol-

---

[3] History.com Editors. "Tokugawa Period and Meiji Restoration." *History.com*, A&E Television Networks, 9 Nov. 2009, www.history.com/topics/japan/meiji-restoration.

[4] Matsumura, Masayoshi, *Baron Kaneko and the Russo-Japanese War*, 2009, Part One, Chapter Four.

lowing his Harvard education, he returned to Japan and was appointed a secretary in the Genroin (National Assembly). Ultimately, it was his diplomatic skill that helped Japan to win the Russo-Japanese War and secure Japan's place as a modern imperial power. Eventually Kaneko became the right-hand man of Prince Ito, the founding father of modern Japan. Having been educated in London, he chaired the bureau that drafted the Meiji Constitution in the 1880s. Trusted deeply by Prince Ito, Kaneko participated in drafting the Constitution which favored the Japanese concept of a kokutai or "national polity" instead of religious preference like the constitutions in the West. It focused on the Japanese identity under the Emperor and fostered a nationalistic pride in the people.

Theodore (Teddy) Roosevelt was also a Harvard graduate and had met Kaneko in 1890 at Roosevelt's Washington home where they were introduced by a mutual Harvard friend. Roosevelt was impressed with Kaneko as he appeared to be Americanized, a titled aristocrat, and a Harvard lawyer. Teddy had never seen Asia, imagined most of the Japanese to be similar to Kaneko, and called Japan "The Yankee of the East". The friendship between Kaneko and Teddy influenced much of the latter's foreign policies, including the outcome of the Russo-Japanese War, which earned him a Nobel Peace Prize.

Japan had attacked Russia in Port Arthur after negotiations broke down over Manchuria and Korea's dominance. China had lost Southern Manchuria to Japan during the First Sino-Japanese War, but Russia had its interest there as well. Although Japan was industrializing, it could not have won the war with Russia without support from the U.S. Due to Kaneko and Roosevelt's relationship, Prince Ito entered the war confident that Roosevelt would be able to intervene if necessary. On April 14, 1904, Roosevelt brought Kaneko to a gathering at the prestigious University Club where they met Wall Street financiers. Within 40 days of the meeting, Wall Street bankers sold millions of dollars in Japanese bonds.

Interestingly, it was also during this war that the Japanese realized that diseases could be as deadly as firepower. Soldiers were suffering from cholera, beri-beri, typhoid fever, and diarrheal diseases. During the siege of Port Arthur, 20,000-25,000 men were sent home from the 80,000 man Third Army.[5] By then Japan had then established its first version of Epidemic Prevention Laboratory.[6]

By the end of the war, Roosevelt was thrilled to negotiate the Treaty of Portsmouth, which handed Korea to Japan. Russia also ceded its interest in Southern Manchuria to Japan as well as the Island of

---

[5] Hawk, Alan, *Military Medicine, The Great Disease Enemy*, p. 333.

[6] Gold, Hal, *Unit 731 Testimony*, p. 22.

Sakhalin. Roosevelt deeply believed that Japan should be the one upholding the Japanese Monroe Doctrine in Asia.

> *"Japan is the only nation in Asia that understands the principles and methods of Western civilization. She has proved that she can assimilate Western civilization, yet not break up her own heritage. All the Asiatic nations are now faced with the urgent necessity of adjusting themselves to the present age. Japan should be their natural leader in that process, and their protector during the transition stage, much as the United States assumed the leadership of the American continent many years ago, and by means of the Monroe Doctrine, preserved the Latin American nations from European interference, while they were maturing their independence."*
> —PRESIDENT THEODORE ROOSEVELT
> TO BARON KENTARO KANEKO,
> JULY 8, 1905.[7]

Manchuria had been special to the rulers of the Qing dynasty who were descendants from that region. In 1905, after the Portsmouth Treaty, the Japanese replaced Russians as leaseholders in the region with

---

[7] Bradley, James, *China Mirage*, p. 60-74.

the Kwantung Garrison and labeled it as Kwantung Leasehold Territory. Throughout the years, the Kwantung Garrison supported various warlords to divide up the power of the Chinese rulers. In 1911, the Kwantung Garrison was involved in campaigns to dismantle the Qing Dynasty who leased them the area. After the 1919 reorganization, the Kwantung Garrison was renamed the Kwantung Army and was separated from the territory's civilian administration. In the early days of Japan's occupation of Manchuria, the Kwantung Army's main duty was to defend Japan's economic interest in Manchuria, including the South Manchuria Railway Zone where the conflict of the Mukden Incident was sparked on September 18, 1931. The Kwantung Army utilized that opportunity to take over Manchuria, rename it Manchukuo, and install Puyi, the last emperor of the Qing Dynasty.

Chapter 2

The Beginning of an Evil Genius

As Japan began its modernization campaign, it relied heavily on science to expand its empire. Born on June 25, 1982 to an established family in the village of Chiyoda-Mura in the Kamo District of Chiba Prefecture, Ishii was a product of his era. As a landowner, he lived a privileged childhood. His primary and secondary schoolmates remembered him as "brash, abrasive, and arrogant." However, since he had a great memory, he was a "teachers' favorite." Raised in the age of Japanese expansionist ambition, Ishii had an ultra-nationalistic desire to be in the military. Less than a month after graduating from the Medical Department of Kyoto Imperial University at age 28, Ishii began his military training as a probation officer in the Third Regiment of the Imperial Guard Division and became a Surgeon-First Lieutenant in less than 6 months. His favorite after work related activity was to visit the red light district of Tokyo for geishas under 15 or 16 years old. Even with a First Lieutenant's minimal pay, he never lacked spending money. During his postgraduate studies at Kyoto Imperial University, Ishii networked eagerly and hustled to climb the career ladder. As a researcher sent to help cure an epidemic that had broken out in Japan, it was then he invented a water filter that could be carried alongside the troops.[8]

He was able to successfully charm the President of Kyoto Imperial University, Araki Torasaburo. He even charmed his daughter, and was able to marry into the family to have a strong backing in medical science. Even with his busy home life, research work, and networking, he still frequented geisha houses and local bars. He eventually stumbled upon the report of the Geneva Protocol and the conference reports of Harada Toyoji and other military doctors and was impressed with the potential of chemical and biological warfare in future war strategy. During World War I, the German army's use of chemical weapons inflicted heavy civilian casualties. Consequently, 44 countries passed an agreement at the 1925 Conference on Disarmament in Geneva on June 17, 1925 and signed an international protocol named "Protocol for the Prohibition of the Use in War of Asphyxiating, Poisonous or

---

[8] Hal Gold, *Unit 731 Testimony*, p. 25.

CHAPTER 2: THE BEGINNING OF AN EVIL GENIUS

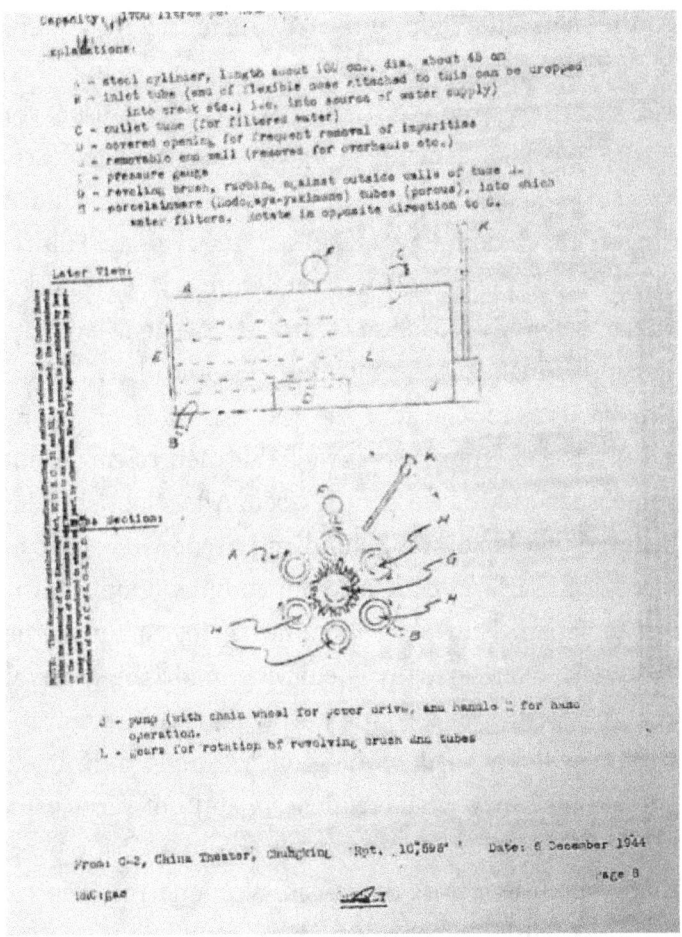

other Gases, and of Bacteriological Methods of Warfare" ("Geneva Protocol"), prohibiting the use of chemical and biological weapons in war. Representatives from Japan were also present at this conference and were involved in drafting and signing the Geneva Protocol, although it was not ratified in Japan at the time.

At the suggestion of his university mentor, Kiyano Kenji, he traveled to 25 Western countries in a span of two years starting from April 1928. It was rather usual for Japanese military members to visit the West to learn, similar to Kaneko's experience. The countries included Singapore, Ceylon, Egypt, Greece, Turkey, Italy, France, Switzerland, Germany, Austria, Hungary, Czechoslovakia, Belgium, Holland, Denmark, Sweden, Norway, Finland, Polance, Soviet Union, Estonia, Latvia, East Prussia, Hawaii, Canada, and the United States. Some countries were more secretive about their research, but some, such as MIT were more open. After the visit, **Ishii believed that Japan was behind and** needed to engage in biological warfare research. Four months upon returning to Japan, Ishii Shiro became an instructor at the Imperial Japanese Army Medical School (IJA Medical School). Japan was a country which lacked mineral resources, which made biological weapons a brilliant choice since they were inexpensive and not very costly to produce or at least that was his argument. Moreover, there were the factors of transmission and the high lethality potential to consider. Therefore, the ultra-nationalistic Ishii Shiro decided to lobby the Army Central, proposing to establish a military agency to develop biological weapons for Japan's national interests. One of his most compelling arguments to his superiors was, "that biological warfare must possess distinct possibilities, otherwise, it would not have been outlawed by the League of Nations."

Chapter 2: The Beginning of an Evil Genius

As usual, Ishii was able to foster connections with others who could advance his career and caught the attention of Koizumi Chikahiko, an ultranationalist serving as Japan's Minister of Health. With his support in August of 1932, an Epidemic Prevention Laboratory headed by Ishii Shiro was approved. However, at the time, the Imperial Japanese Army Medical School already had an Epidemic Prevention Laboratory.

In Tokyo, Ishii experienced tremendous success with Koizumi's support. He was able to secure a 1795 square meter complex at the Army Medical College. Since many of his peers were antagonized by him, he was greatly concerned about conducting research at Japan's capital at the time. There was no way he could capture human experimental subjects for vaccine and defensive research work. The type of work which Ishii wanted to do needed to be done outside of Japan proper and the territory of Manchuria looked perfect. In the summer of 1932, after Ishii and his childhood friend, Masuda Tomosada, took a tour to Harbin, Ishii saw Manchuria as a perfect place for his scientific advancement.[9]

---

[9] Harris, Sheldon, *Factories of Death*, p. 15-21.

Chapter 3

A Beta Testing Site

Harbin, located in Northern Manchuria, was a culture hub in the 1930s. A trading port and very diverse city, religions practiced there included Buddhism, Taoism, Shintoism, Islam, Judaism, Catholicism, Christianity, and Russian Orthodoxy. Due to the Russian influence, architecturally, Harbin resembled more of a European city with cobbled stone streets, department stores, and the presence of European artists. As with most "Concession" cities in Imperial China, Harbin was divided into three areas—the industrial area where the desperately poor lived, the middle class Chinese area, and the "Russian Concession" where Western foreigners, Japanese, and well to do Chinese lived.

Although it was not as superficially attractive as operating a human experimentation facility in the middle of Tokyo, Harbin was still too cosmopolitan for any biological warfare research to go unnoticed. Since human experimentation was against international law, Ishii had to find a place that provided maximum secrecy. He chose a place in the Nan Gang District, a seedy district in Beiyinhe, a village about 70 kilometers southeast of Harbin, and began conducting human experiments.

One day in 1932, Ishii and the Japanese army entered the village and evacuated the whole block where Xuan Hua and Wu Miao intersected. They occupied a multi-use structure which had supported 100 Chinese vendors selling clothes and food to the local villagers and set up a temporary site for large-scale human experimentation. They then drafted Chinese laborers to construct the Zhong Ma complex to house the Togo Unit. Ishii named it after Togo Heihachiro, who was one of his favorite war heroes and the greatest naval strategist who brought Japan victory over Russia during the Russo-Japanese War. The Chinese laborers were underpaid and constantly watched by guards, limiting their movements and preventing them from seeing what was happening in the complex. The complex was completed in one year and had 100 rooms, 3-meter-high brick walls and a surrounding electric fence. One thousand captives at a time were imprisoned. To ensure secrecy, security guards patrolled the complex 24 hours a day every day. Saburō Endō, Director of Operations of the Kwantung Army, once inspected the "Tōgō Unit." In his book, "*The Fifteen Years' Sino-Japanese War and Me*", he described it as follows:

> [It was] converted from a rather large soy sauce workshop, surrounded by high rammed earth wall. All the attending military doctors had pseudonyms, and they were strictly regulated and were not allowed to communicate with the outsiders. The name of the unit was "Tōgō Unit." One by one, the subjects of the experiments were imprisoned in a sturdy iron lattice and inoculated with various pathogenic bacteria to observe changes in their conditions. They used prisoners on death row in the prisons of Harbin for these experiments. It was said that it was for national defense purposes, but the experiments were performed with appalling brutality. The dead were burned in high-voltage electric furnaces, leaving no trace.[10]

There was hearsay about the complex's interior. A local from the region stated the following, "We heard rumors of people having blood drawn in there but we never went near the place. We were too afraid. When the construction started, there were about forty houses in our village, and a lot of people were driven out. About one person from each home

---

[10] *Japan-China Book Publisher*, 1974, p. 162.

was taken to work on the construction. People were gathered from villages from all around here, maybe about a thousand people in all. The only things we worked on were the surrounding wall and the earthen walls. The Chinese that worked on the buildings were brought in from somewhere, but we didn't know where. After everything was finished, those people were killed."

Despite its secrecy, the word still got out that prisoners were being taken from Chinese Communists as well as other "bandits" and other suspicious people who were then subjected to tests. One such test was to drain gradually the victims' blood to see if death occurred from the lack of blood.[11] The unit drew 500 cc of blood from each prisoner every 3-5 days. As their bodies grew weaker, they were dissected for further research. An average prisoner lasted a maximum of a month.

Due to brutal winters faced by the Kwantung Army, they needed to find the best method for treating frostbite and increase their productivity. Ishii's team gathered human subjects and subjected them to freezing and unfreezing in very cold weather. The experiments sometimes included observing test subjects whose limbs had been frozen and then severed. The team reported to General Okamura Yasuji, De-

---

[11] Gold, Hal, *Unit 731 Testimony*, p. 36.

Chapter 3: A Beta Testing Site

puty Commander in Chief of the Kwantung Army between 1933-1934, that the best way to treat frostbite was to soak a limb in water at 37 degrees Celsius. This conclusion was reached after limbs of the logs were frozen every year in Ishii's Unit. According to the December 28 testimony of witness Furuichi at the Khabarovsk Trial, "Experiments in freezing human beings were performed every year in the detachment, in the coldest months of the year—November, December, January and February. The experimental technique was as follows: the test subjects were taken out into the frost at about 11 o'clock at night, compelled to dip their hands into a barrel of cold water and forced to stand with wet hands in the frost for a long time. Alternatively, some were taken out dressed, but with bare feet and compelled to stand at night in the frost during the coldest period of the year. When frostbite had developed, the subjects were taken to a room and forced to put their feet in water of 5 degrees Celsius, after which the temperature was gradually increased."

Witness Kurakazu, who was Sergeant Major in Unit 731 from 1940 and taken prisoner in August 1945 by the Soviet Troop in Harbin, stated on August 8, 1939 during the Khabarovsk Trial, "I saw experiments performed on living people for the first time in December 1940. I was shown these experiments by researcher Yoshimura, a member of the 1st

Division. These experiments were performed in the prison laboratory. When I walked into the prison laboratory, five Chinese experimentees were sitting there; two of these Chinese had no fingers at all, their hands were black; in those of three others the bones were visible. They had fingers, but they were only bones. Yoshimura told me that this was the result of freezing experiments."[12]

According to Major Karasawa during the Khabarovsk Trial, Ishii was curious about using plague as weapons in war and captured plague infected mice to test on subjects in the Zhong Ma complex. "Ishii told me that he had experimented with cholera and plague on the mounted bandits of Manchuria during 1933-1934 and discovered that the plague was effective."

According to Lt. General Endo Saburo's diary entry on November 16, 1933 at the Zhong Ma complex, "The second squad which was responsible for poison gas, liquid poison; and the First Squad which was responsible for electrical experiments. Two bandits were used by each squad for the experiments.

1. Phosgene gas—5-minute injection of gas into a brick-lined room; the subject was still alive one day after inhalation of gas; critically ill with pneumonia.

---

[12] *Khabarovsk Trial*, p. 295.

2. Potassium cyanide—the subject was injected with 15 mg.; subject lost consciousness approximately 20 minutes later.
3. 20,000 volts—several jolts were not enough to kill the subject; injection of poison required to kill the subject.
4. 5000 volts—several jolts were not enough; after several minutes of continuous current, subject was burned to death."

Word must have reached the Japanese scientific community; the New Japan Medicine Report published in 1934 stated, "The Ninth General Japan Medical Conference is a big event on this small archipelago in the Far East. Japan's medicine is now independent from the medical community of the world. We have already been ousted from the League of Nations [;] it is the feeling of the people that in the field of science, others will look up to Japan".

The Tōgō Unit established a strict security system to keep its research highly confidential. Surprisingly, during the Mid-Autumn Festival on the 15th day of the 8th lunar month in 1934, 16 Chinese prisoners escaped from prison, making it difficult for the Tōgō Unit to sustain confidentiality at the Zhong Ma location.

基本動作、應用動作ニ關スル學術ヲ教育シ剛健ナル氣力、體力ヲ養成シ白兵ノ使用ニ習熟セシム

第四章 成績報告

第二十五條 本教則第八條ニ據リ教官ニ甲種、乙種並丙種學生ニ就キ試驗ヲ實施シ其成績ハ點數ヲ以テ之ヲ示シ擔任課目教育終了後二週間以內（最終教育課目ニ在リテハ教育終了三週間前）ニ關係教育主任（教官）ヨリ又甲種學生ノ專攻成績ハ各擔任教官ヨリ教育終了三週間前ニ校長ニ提出スルモノトス
校長ハ前項ノ成績ヲ點查綜合シ列序ヲ附ス

第二十六條 學生ノ教育狀況ハ教育終了後直ニ教育主任（教官）ヨリ之ヲ校長ニ提出シ校長ハ教育終了後一ケ月以內ニ敎育實施ノ概況ヲ醫務局長ヲ經テ陸軍大臣ニ報告ス

左記

內科學敎室ニ於テハ前年一月軍陣內ノ大使命トシテ軍隊結核ニ關スル各種ノ研究ヲ課セラレ、之ガ早期發見、豫防ヲ急務トシテ研究實施ニ移リ、敎官中村軍醫監主宰ノ下ニ東京第一衞戍病院看護兵ニ就キ調査研究ヲ實施セシガ、之ガ研究ハ現下ニ於ケル國軍衞生上ノ焦眉ノ急務タルニ鑑ミ、更ニ本年三月改メテ三木軍醫正ノ主宰ノ下ニ內科學敎室職員全員ハ東京第一衞戍病院內科病室及兵舍關係職員ノ熱心ナル協力ヲ得テ同病院看護兵ニ精細ナル檢查ヲ實施シ、更ニ十月伊吹軍醫正ヲ主任トシテ近衞師團兵ニ就キ同樣ノ研究調査ヲ果セリ。

昭和六年乃至九年事變ニ於ケル滿洲事變ノ功績ニ關シテハ昭和九年三月三十一日ヲ以テ功績調査ノ締切日ト定メラレタリ以テ、各關係ニ就キ調査了ツヘキ功績上申中ノ處、本校高等官職員ニシテ昭和七年九月十六日ヨリ同十一年八月三十一日ニ至ル間ニ於テ行賞發令セラレタル有學位者學校長以下七十九名アリ。行賞ノ發令ハ昭和九年四月二十九日附ニシテ敍賜ト同日附ニ以テ夫々昭和六年乃至九年事變從軍記章ヲ授與セラレタリ。

本年中本校職員ニシテ戰死竝殉職セシ者左記四名アリ。

Chapter 3: A Beta Testing Site

本籍　千葉縣山武郡千代田村大里加茂一四五一

屬託　田下五郎　明治四十二年四月一日生

昭和十年七月十八日滿洲國濱江省雙城縣藍機子溝（背陰河東南方約四粁）ニ於テ匪賊討伐中左胸部穿透性貫通銃創ヲ受ケ戰死。

本籍　千葉縣山武郡千代田村大里加茂一四五一

屬託　田下丑之助　大正二年九月十一日生

昭和十年六月五日滿洲國濱江省雙城縣李家瓦房（背陰河東南方三粁）ニ於テ匪賊討伐中頭部貫通銃創ヲ受ケ戰死。

本籍　千葉縣山武郡千代田村大里一二一五

雇員　萩原豊　大正八年三月二十四日生

昭和十年六月二十五日腸チフスニ罹リ同月二十九日東京第二衛戍病院ニ入院同年七月二十九日死亡。

本籍　秋田縣南秋田郡土崎港町清水町六〇

雇員　渡邊綱吉　明治四十一年一月二十八日生

昭和十年六月二十四日腸チフスニ罹リ同日東京第二衛戍病院ニ入院同年七月二十六日死亡。

十二月二十七日午後二時ヨリ築地本願寺ニ於テ壯嚴裡ニ葬儀並慰靈祭ヲ執行セリ。

昭和十一年

Catching a guard drunk, a prisoner named Li took the opportunity to smash a bottle on the guard's head and snatch the keys. Of the 16 Chinese people who escaped, four died due to the cold, hunger, or conditions contracted at the Togo Unit. Twelve fled to the Third Route Army of the Northeast Anti-Japanese United Army. After learning about the situation, the Third Route Army attacked the Tōgō Unit in Beiyinhe. Within a year, the Zhong Ma complex exploded. Although short lived, the complex served the purpose of confirming Ishii's beliefs as well as showing his military superior the types of research he was capable of conducting.

Chapter 4

Establishing Pingfan

With the Zhong Ma Complex destroyed, Ishii needed a better structure. Since the Togo Unit had been supporting Ishii's biological weapon research promises, the budget for his unit increased. On May 30th, 1936, the Togo Unit, led by Ishii Shiro, was awarded the "Army Regulation 'A' No. 7" by the Emperor and became an official army unit. Therefore, it was no longer an agency part of the Epidemic Prevention Institute of the Army Military Medical School but actually was under the Kwantung Army as Central Epidemic Prevention and Water Purification Department of the Kwantung Army with the headquarters located at Pingfan, closer to the city of Harbin. The initial budget was 3 million yen for personnel, 200 to 300 thousand yen per autonomous unit and 6 million yen for experimentation and research. Hence, the annual budget of over 10 million yen for Pingfan was huge at the time. It was a short train ride away via the South Manchuria Railway.

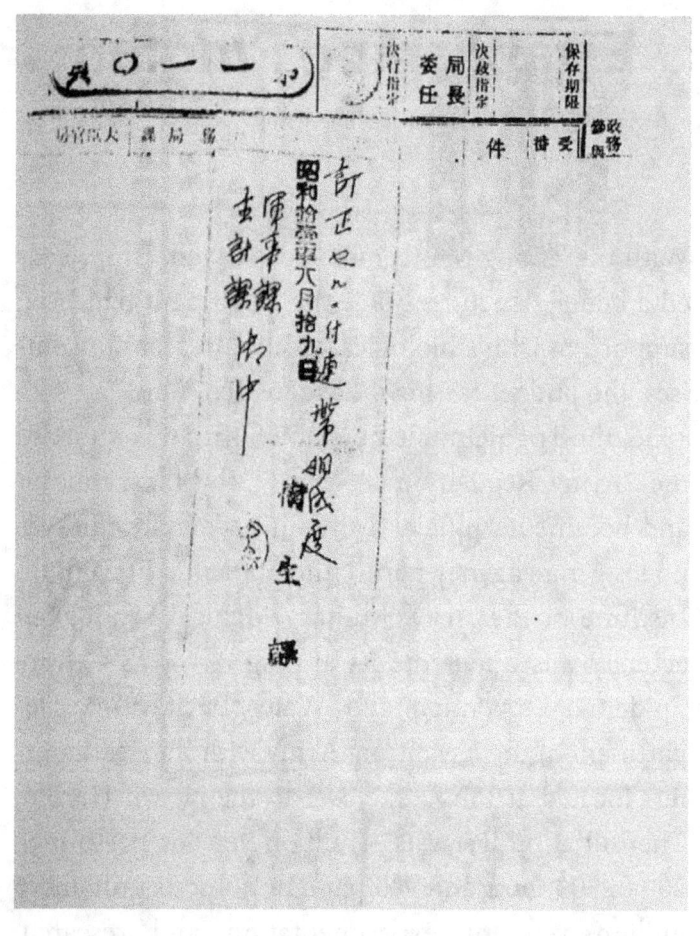

Chapter 4: Establishing Pingfan

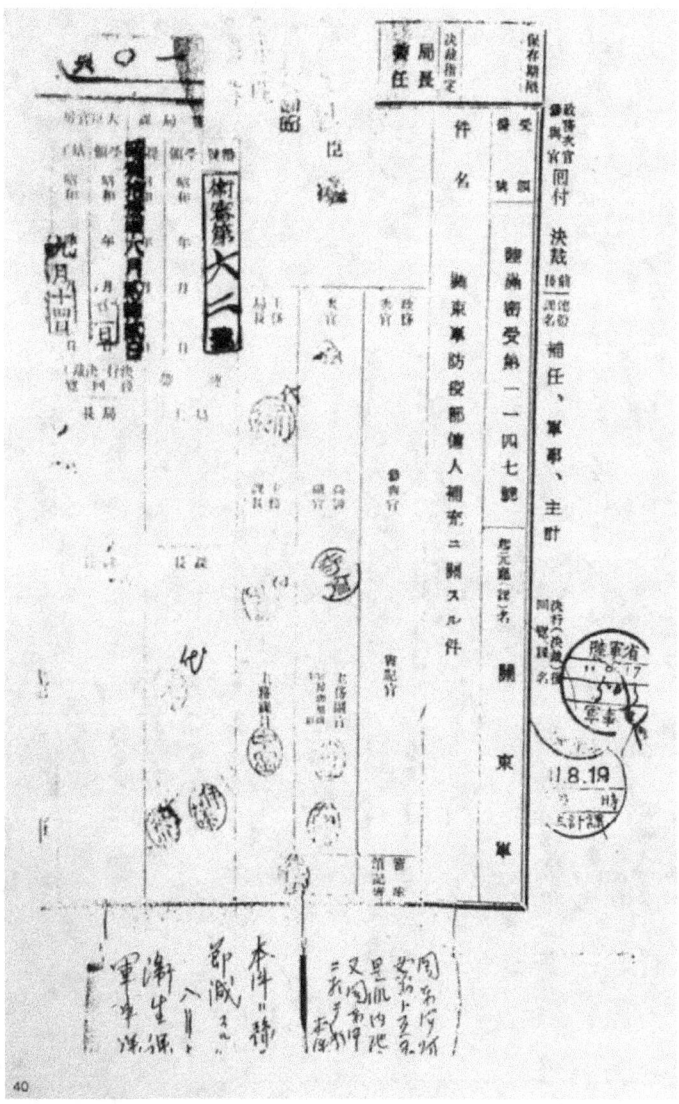

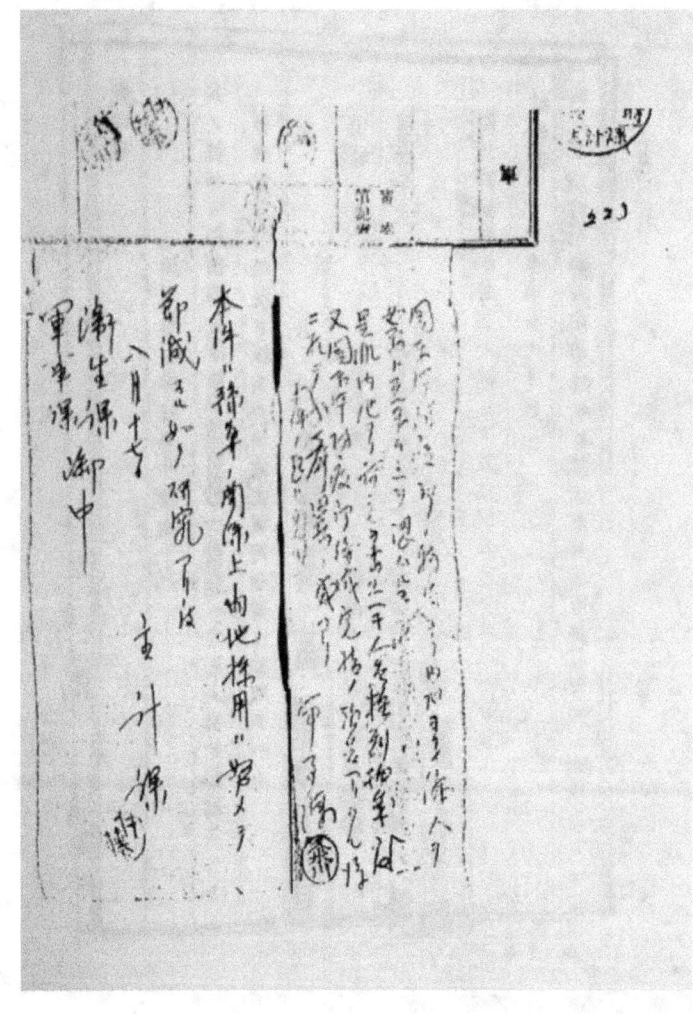

Chapter 4: Establishing Pingfan

陸満密

陸軍軍医学校長ヘ達案

其ノ校ヨリ臨時衛生部編成要員トシテ軍医以下軍属ニ至ル左記人員ヲ配属スヘシ
但到着日時場所ニ関シテハ関東軍司令官ト協議スヘシ

左記

軍医 五十名

干部人 三十八名

陸満密第三二七号 昭和十一年 八月廿二日

陸満密

大官ヨリ関東軍参謀長ヘ通牒案

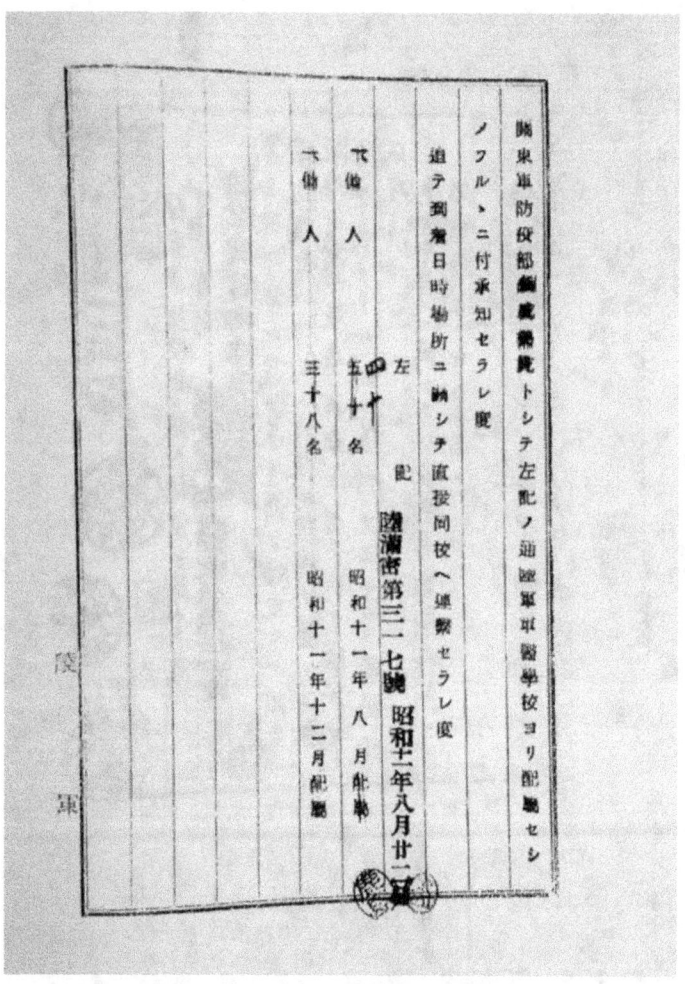

Chapter 4: Establishing Pingfan

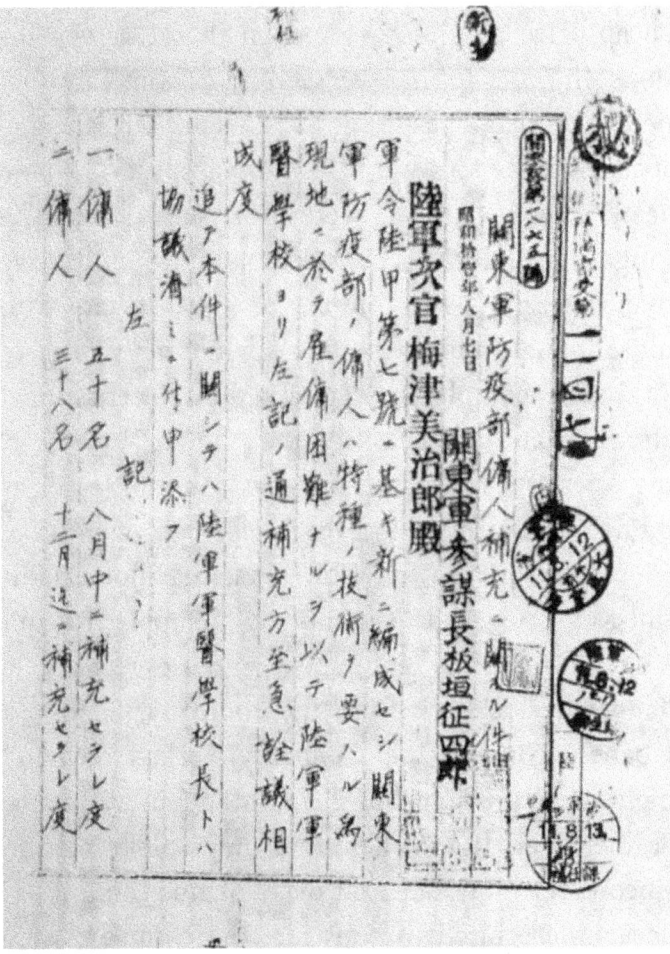

Similar to the Zhong Ma structure, Pingfan was evacuated by the Japanese Army. Hundreds of families were forced to move out and sell their land at a cheap price despite having been there for generations. In order to increase secrecy this time around, people needed a pass to go to Pingfan. Even the airspace over the area was off-limits except to Japanese army planes. Violators were to be shot down. The Pingfan complex was considerably more impressive than the Zhong Ma complex as a walled city with more than 70 buildings on a six kilometer tract of land. The complex's huge size drew international attention and when asked what the structure was, the scientists replied that it was a lumber mill as human subjects were logs, or in Japanese, "maruta"s.

Abusing his power, Ishii granted Nihon Tokushu-Kogyo Co. Ltd. A monopoly to supply the unit with all necessary equipment and he received a handsome kickback from the company. Suzuki, a Japanese construction company, worked day and night when possible, but due to Manchuria's weather, there were times when it was impossible to do so since everything had iced over. Again, Chinese laborers were hired to construct the complex, were denied any basic human rights and wore rags even during cold weather. Some died from the cold and were tossed into a pit, their clothes and valuables passed on to the next laborers who needed them.

The laborers slept in tents that barely sheltered them from the winter and meals consisted of pickled vegetables and dumplings. The attitude toward the Chinese laborers and subjects of experiments was similar. Since there were so many Chinese, it did not matter if one or two died because there would always be others.[13]

At the time, the Imperial Japanese Army internally referred to the unit related to Ishii's biological warfare as the Ishii Network and referred to Pingfan as the network's headquarters, since there were other research centers related to Unit 731. The following are some known research centers related to Ishii's Network and when they were established.

- The Army's Noborito Laboratory was established (1937)
- The Central Epidemic Prevention and Water Purification Department of the North China Army/ Unit 1855 was established (1938)
- The Central Epidemic Prevention and Water Purification Department of Central China/ Unit 1644 (1939)
- The Guangzhou Epidemic Prevention and Water Purification Department of South China Army/ Unit 8604 (1942)

---

[13] Harris, Sheldon, *Factories of Death*, p. 38-39.

- The Central Epidemic Prevention and Water Purification Department of the Southern Expeditionary Army/ Unit 9620 (1942).

Human experimentation was not only done in Ishii's Network. According to Kawashima who served as Chief of the General Division from April 1939 to March 1943, by order of the Japanese Minister for War, Unit 731 had a 10 million yen budget in 1940 alone with 5 million yen to be spent on experimental work by the order of the Emperor.[14]

At one point, anyone working in the medical research field was working for the Ishii Network. The impression of the medical field was one of good intentions, but under the ultra-nationalistic agenda, the scientists who had good intentions turned to producing weapons against humanity. If a scientist opposed Unit 731, he had no future in the field. Ishii regularly made speeches to convince his peers what they were doing in Unit 731 was good for humanity and regularly gave speeches to recruit young microbiologists and other potential technical recruits at several Army medical colleges throughout Japan as well as Kyoto Imperial University and Tokyo Imperial University. In one of the speeches, he stated, "Our God given mission as doctors is to challenge all varieties of diseases causing micro-organism; to

---

[14] *Khabarovsk Trial, December 25th Examination of Accused Kawashima.*

block all roads of intrusion into the human body; to annihilate all foreign matter resident in our bodies; and to devise the most expeditious treatment possible. However, the research work upon which we are now about to embark is the completely opposite of these principles, and may cause us some anguish as doctors. Nevertheless, I beseech you to pursue this research, based on the dual thrill of (1), a scientist to exert efforts to probing for the truth in natural science and research into, and discovery of, the unknown world and (2), as a military person to successfully build a powerful military weapon against the enemy."[15]

Sometimes in the same speeches, he used charts, slides, and even 8mm motion picture films of his human experimentation work.[16] By 1942, Ishii was overloaded with responsibilities and made Lieutenant General Masaji Kitano the 2nd commander of Unit 731.[17]

One could discern the activities of Unit 731, the Ishii's Network's headquarters, by checking out the map unearthed by the Soviet Union during the Khabarovsk Trial in the Materials on the Trial of Former Servicemen of the Japanese Army Charged with Manufacturing and Employing Bacteriological Weapons.

---

[15] Quoted in Tsuneishi, *The Germ Warfare Unit That Disappeared*, p. 71.
[16] Harris, Sheldon, *Factories of Death*, p. 58.
[17] Gold, Hal, *Unit 731 Testimony*, p. 60.

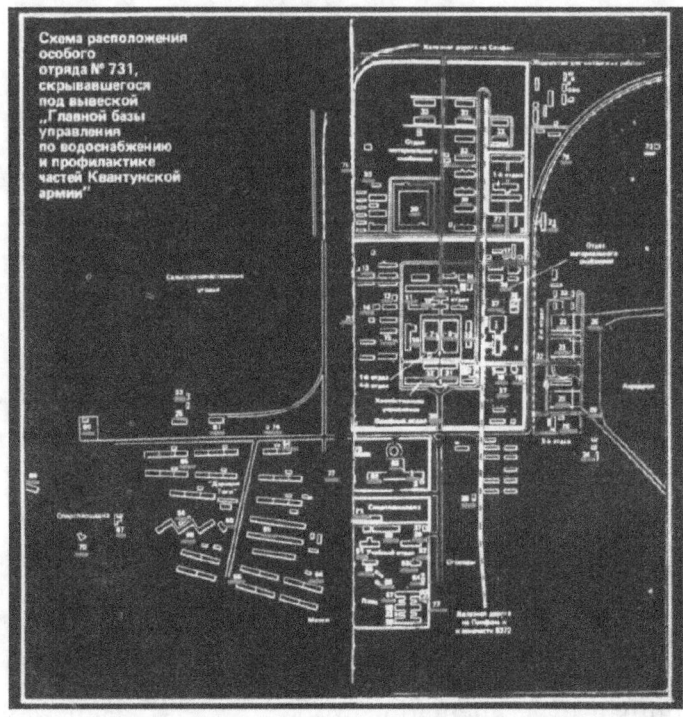

Translation: Map of the location of special unit No. 731, hiding under the sign "The Main Base of the Department of Water Supply and Prevention of the Kwantung Army Units."

Translation: Breakdown of the map

- Commercial management. The 1st division, the 4th division, the medical corridor, Central corridor.
- 1st floor. The 4th division. Groups: Karasawa (production of bacteria); Asashina (the study of typhus and production of vaccinations)
- 2nd floor. The 1st division. Groups: Ishimura (the study of frostbite); Minato (the study of cholera); Ejima (the study of dysentery); Ota (the study of anthrax); Okamoto and Ishikawa (the study of pathogenesis); Utime (the study of blood serums).
- 3rd floor. First division. Groups: Tanabe (the study of typhus); Futaka (the study of tuberculosis); Kusami (pharmacological studies)

CHAPTER 4: ESTABLISHING PINGFAN

Пояснения к схеме

Хозяйственное управление. 1-й отдел, 4-й отдел. Лечебный отдел. Центральный коридор.

1-й этаж. 4-й отдел. Группы: Карасава (производство бактерий); Асахина (исследование сыпного тифа и производство вакцины).

2-й этаж. 1-й отдел. Группы: Иосимура (исследование обморожения); Минато (исследование колеры); Эдзима (исследование дизентерии); Оота (исследование сибирской язвы); Окамото и Исикава (исследование патогенеза); Утими (исследование сыворотки крови).

3-й этаж. 1-й отдел. Группы: Танабэ (исследование тифа); Футаки (исследование туберкулеза); Кусами (фармакологические исследования).

Под цифрами

1. 1-й этаж. Лечебница, административно-хозяйственные органы.

2-й этаж. „Выставочная комната" (образцы различных частей человеческого тела, отражающие результаты „исследований"), конференц-зал, „комната усопших", кабинет начальника отряда, бухгалтерия, канцелярия, плановый отдел.

2. 1-й этаж. Почта, телеграф, административно-хозяйственные органы, библиотека.

2-й этаж. Классы для практических занятий.

3. Книгохранилище. 4. Группа Танака (исследование насекомых). 5. Группа Иосимура (исследование обморожения), холодильная камера. 6. Хозяйственные помещения. 7. „Бревна", группа Арита (рентгеновская съемка). 8. „Бревна". 9. Группа Касахара (исследование вирусов). 10. Группа Така-

хаси (исследование чумы). 11. Секционный зал (помещение для патологоанатомических вскрытий). 12. Печь для сжигания трупов. 13. Виварий спецгруппы. 14. Комната забора крови. 15. Конюшни. 16. Группа Ногути (исследование риккетсий). 17. Группа инженерных работ. 18. Газораспределительная камера. 19. Газгольдер. 20. Караульное помещение.

2-й отдел.

21. Метеогруппа. 22. Авиагруппа. 23. Ангары. 24. Радиогруппа. 25. Группа Ягисава (исследование растений). 26. Взлетно-посадочная полоса. 27. Гаражи.

3-й отдел.

28. Транспортная группа.

Отдел материального снабжения.

30. Блок „ро" (хранилище вакцины, стерильные холодильные камеры и термокамеры, термокамеры высокой температуры, канцелярия, гараж).

31—38. Административно-хозяйственные помещения. (Объектов под номерами 39—49 на схеме нет, так как они находились в Харбине).

Учебный отдел.

50—59. Учебные и административно-хозяйственные органы и помещения.

„Деревня Того".

60. Синтоистский храм. 61—71, 73—74. Жилые и хозяйственно-бытовые помещения для сотрудников отряда. 72. Газовая камера. 75. Ограждения из колючей проволоки. 76. Земляной вал. Ров без воды. Ток высокого напряжения. 77. Земляной вал. Ров без воды.

Under the numbers:

1. 1st floor. Hospital, administrative-commercial organs.
2nd floor. "Exhibition room" (samples of various human body parts, reflecting the results of "studies"), conference hall, "room of the dead", office of the boss of the unit, bookkeeping, stationary, planning unit.
2. 1st floor. Mail center, telegraph, administrative-commercial organs, library
2nd floor. Classrooms for practice lessons.
3. Book depository
4. Group Tanaka (study of bugs)
5. Group Ishimura (study of frostbite), refrigerating chamber
6. Utilities room
7. "Logs," group Arita (x-ray surveys)
8. "Logs"
9. Group Kazahara (the study of viruses)
10. Group Takahashi (the study of the plague)
11. Autopsy room (accommodations for post-mortem autopsies)
12. Oven for burning corpses
13. Special group vivariums
14. Room for the sampling of blood
15. Barn
16. Group Naguti (the study of rickets)
17. Group of engineer work
18. Gas distribution chamber
19. Gas tank
20. Guard accommodations

2nd Division
21. Experimentations
22. Air groups
23. Hangers
24. Radio group
25. Group Yagisawa (the study of plants)
26. Runway
27. Garages

3rd Division
28. Transportation group.

The division of material supply
30. Block "Ro" (vaccination storage, sterile refrigeration chambers and heat chambers, high temperature heat chambers, stationary, garage)

31-38. Administrative-commercial rooms.
(There are no objects under the numbers 39-49 on the map because they were located in Harbin).

Training division
50-59. Training and administrative-commercial organs and accommodations.

"The village of Togo"
60. Shinto Temple.
61-71, 73-74. Living residencies and management-household accommodations for employees of the unit.
72. Gas chamber
75. Barbed wire fences
76. Earthen shaft. Trench without water. A high-current voltage.
77. Earthen shaft. Trench without water.

Chapter 5

Experiences at the Human Experimentation Complex

The buildings in number 7 and 8, nicknamed "Ro" and "Ha", were very important since they housed the logs and were heavily guarded to ensure secrecy. Building 7 housed male victims while building 8 housed females and children. Depending on the type of research for which a victim was needed, the cell had either single or multiple occupants. Buildings 7 and 8 were designed to house 400 inmates, but most believe that an average of 200 inmates were housed at any given time. Each cell had windows near the floor to make it easier to draw blood samples and walls were 30-40 centimeters thick. The cells were kept clean to ensure the quality of research and each cell even had a flushing toilet.[18]

---

[18] Gold, Hal, *Unit 731 Testimony*, p. 40.

Victims normally were brought to Pingfan in the dead of night in crammed freight cars with lumber logs on top or were delivered in grayish-green paneled Dodge trucks owned by the Kempeitai. The victims were then brought into the building via a secret tunnel. According to a witness, Fang Shen Yu, technicians in white coats handled the victims who were tied in bags so tightly that their head and feet touched each other.[19] The way to secure victims was similar to the method of securing victims in the Zhong Ma Complex, but on a larger scale at Pingfan. Anyone charged with any type of crime such as anti-Japanese sentiment, opium smoking, espionage, communism, mental handicap or homelessness was sent to Unit 731 for experiments. Victims included mainly Chinese, stateless White Russians, Harbin Jews, Soviet prisoners captured at the borders, Mongolians, Koreans, and Europeans accused of espionage. During the Khabarovsk Trial, Major Iijima Yoshio admitted that he was personally responsible for subjecting at least 40 Soviet citizens to certain human experiments. The Chief of the Kwantung Army Kempeitai, Major General Shirokura, had issued Operational Order 224, which sent 30 prisoners to Unit 731.[20]

---

[19] Harris, Sheldon, *Factories of Death*, p. 49.
[20] *Khabarovsk Trial*, Vol. 6, p. 242.

Chapter 5: Experiences at the Human Experimentation Complex

Attachment to the notice from the chief of the division of police services headquarter of the Kwantung gendarmerie: a list with instructions for the categories of persons, sent in the order "special delivery."

The pictures depict the full Operational Order no. 224 of the Kwantung gendarmerie on the massive "special delivery". The memo reads,

Head of the Kwantung gendarmerie,
General-Major Shirakura

Order

OPERATIONAL ORDER no. 1 OF THE
GENDARMERIE UNIT HIRANO
Order according to the Hirano Unit
Training division of the Kwantung gendarmerie
August 8th. 17 O'clock

1. The second "special transportation," held on the basis of the operating order of the Kwantung gendarmerie no. 222, is produced in agreement to paragraph 1 of the operational order of the Kwantung gendarmerie no. 224, Page 47
2. Unit Hirano will protect the "special transportation" with part of their forces.
3. Field officer Imamura is leading 24 gendarmes (named in the appendix) and one noncommissioned officer medic will immediately leave from Xinjin and on arrival in Shanhaiguan will receive orders from the

Ji-zhou gendarmerie unit. Before departure, will be received from the headquarters of the Kwantung gendarmerie means to accompany the arrested (81 leg shackles, 52 hand shackles, 40 ropes for binding during detention, 25 ropes for binding during escorting) and from the Mukden gendarmerie unit will be received 30 hand shackles and 40 ropes for tying up prisoners during escorting.
4. Supply in transit with a fifty percent surcharge based on table. 5 temporary allowance rules are made in Manchuria at the expense of the Kwantung gendarmerie.
5. In other matters, follow the operational order no. 222 of the Kwantung gendarmerie.

Leader of the unit
Captain
Hirano

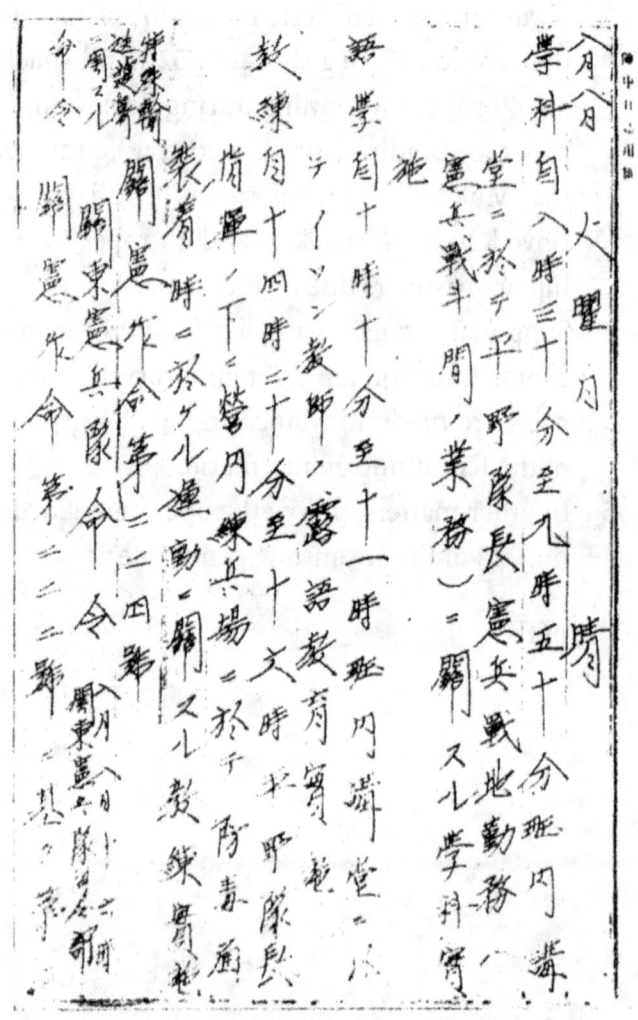

Оперативный приказ № 224 квантунской жандармерии о массовой «особой отправке», стр. 1.

Арх. дело № 845, стр. 45.

Оперативный приказ № 224 квантунской жандармерии
о массовой «особой отправке», стр. 2.

Арх. дело № 845, стр. 45 — продолжение.

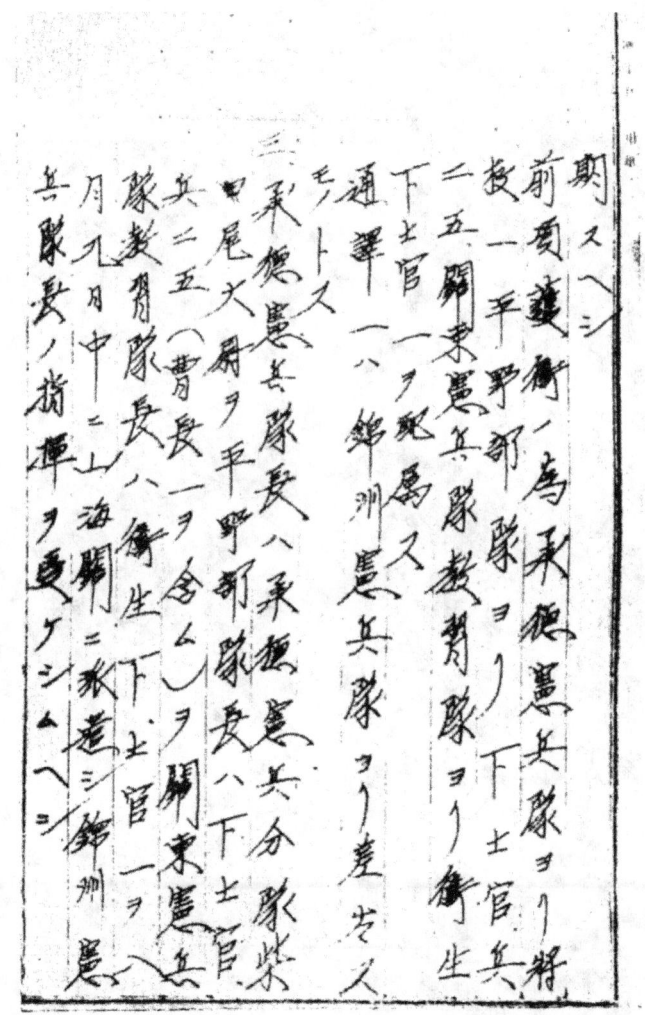

Оперативный приказ № 224 квантунской жандармерии о массовой «особой отправке», стр. 3.

Арх. дело № 845, стр. 46.

Chapter 5: Experiences at the Human Experimentation Complex

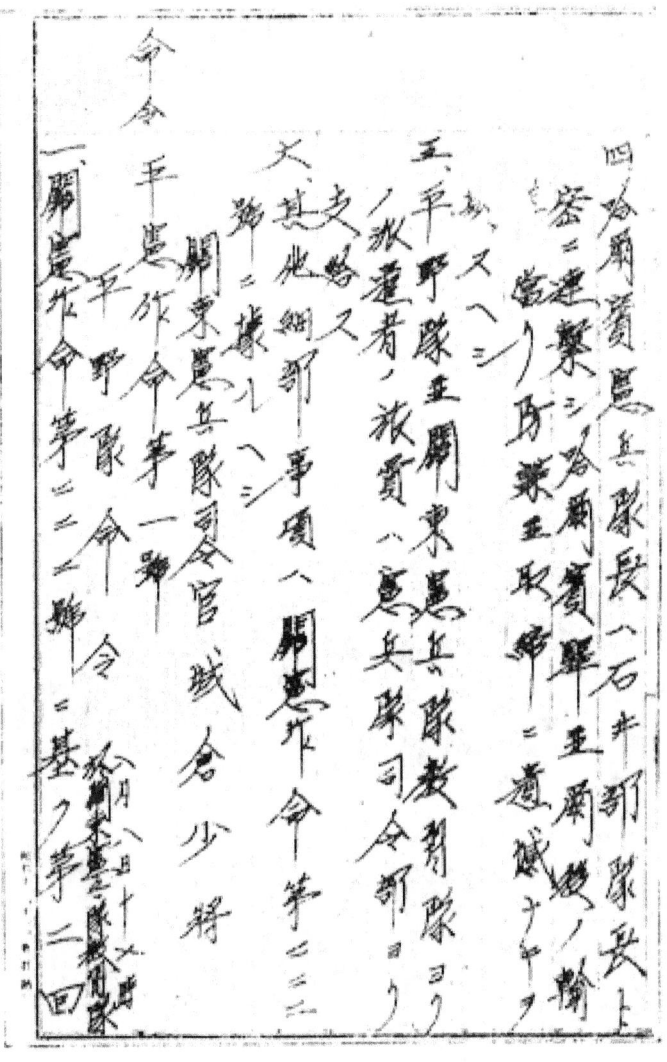

Оперативный приказ № 224 квантунской жандармерии
о массовой «особой отправке»
и оперативный приказ № 1 по отряду Хирано.
Арх. дело № 845, стр. 44 – продолжение.

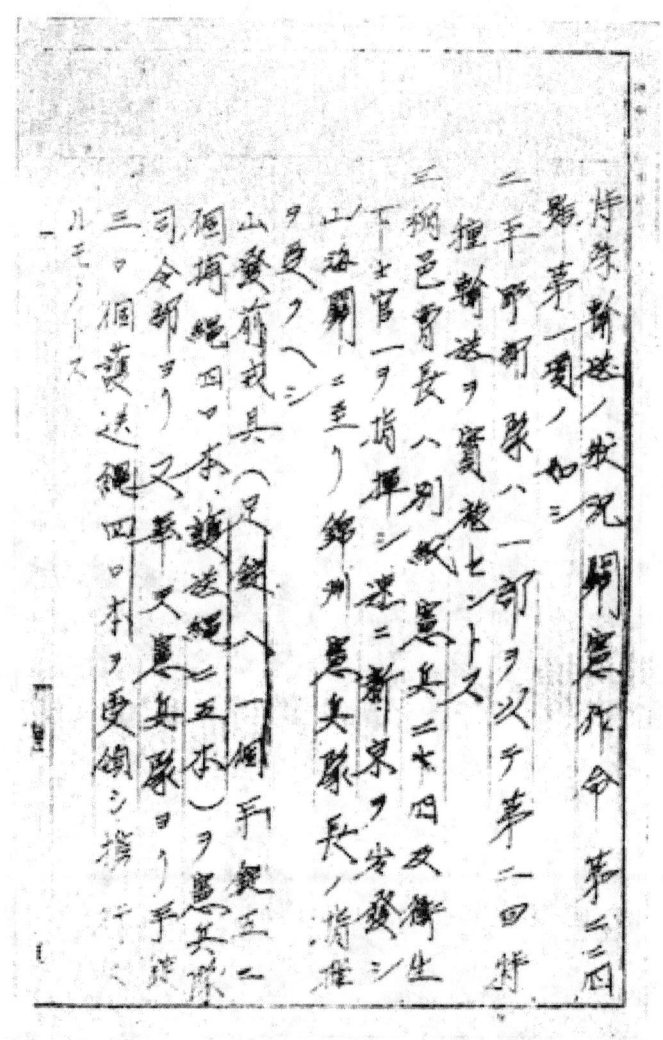

Оперативный приказ № 1 по отряду Хирано
о массовой «особой отправке».

Арх. дело № 845, стр. 47.

CHAPTER 5: EXPERIENCES AT THE HUMAN EXPERIMENTATION COMPLEX

The diversity of prisoners ensured the reliability of the research data. Each prisoner was assigned a number that started with 101 and ended at 1500. Once 1500 was reached, they began again at 101, which made it impossible to determine how many actually fell victim to Unit 731.[21] No one was allowed to survive Unit 731 alive. "If a prisoner survived the inoculation of lethal bacteria, this did not save him from repeated experiments, which were continued until death from infection supervened. The infected victims were given medical treatment in order to test various methods of restoring soundness. They were fed normally and, after full recovery, were used for the next experiment and infected with another type of germ. Ultimately, no one ever left this death factory alive.[22]

Since Unit 731 had been labelled a lumber mill to the locals, most either did not worry about the complex or were too afraid to do so. The role of prison warden was assigned to Ishii's own brother, Mitsuo, to ensure no secret leaked out.[23]

A researcher named Ueda Yataro later recalled his experience with a maruta who shared a cell with four other victims. "He was already too weak to stand. The heavy leg irons bit at his legs. When he moved, they

---

[21] Morimura, *Devil's Gluttony* Vol 3.
[22] *Khabarovsk Trial*, Vol 3, p. 60.
[23] Tsuneishi, *The Germ Warfare that Disappeared*, p. 48.

made a full, clanking sound. His fellow cellmates sat around him and watched him. Nobody spoke. The water in the toilet was running with an ominous sound. In the corridor outside the cell, the guards stood with their pistols strapped on. The commander of the guards also was there. The man's screams of death had no effect on them. This was an everyday occurrence. There was nothing special. To these guards, the people in here have already lost all rights. Their names have been exchanged for just a number written across the front of their shirts and the name maruta. They are referred to only as 'Maruta Number X.' They are counted not as one person or two persons but "one log, two logs." We are not concerned with where they are from, how they came here. The man looked like a farmer, covered with grime. He was wasting away, and his cheekbones protruded. His eyes glared out from the dirt and tattered cotton clothes he was wrapped in. The team leader was fully pleased with yesterday's results. We never had such a typical change in blood picture and rate of infection, and I was eagerly looking forward to see what changes would be present in today's blood sample. With high hopes, I came to the Number 7 cell block with the armed guards at my side. The maruta I was working on was on the verge of death. It would be disastrous if he died. Then I would not be able to get a blood sample, and we would not obtain the important results of

Chapter 5: Experiences at the Human Experimentation Complex

the tests we had been working on. I called his number. No answer came. I motioned through the window at the other four prisoners to bring him over. They sat there without moving. I screamed abusively at them to hurry up and bring him over to the window. One of the guards pulled out a gun, aimed it at them and screamed in Chinese. Resigned, they gently lifted up the other man and brought him over to the window. More important to me than the man's death was the blood flowing in the human guinea pig's body at the moment just before his death. His hand was purplish and turning cold. He put his arm through the opening. I was elated. Filled with a sense of victory and holding down my inexpressible excitement, thinking forward to how the team leader would be waiting for these results, I reached for the hypodermic. I inserted the needle into the vein. It made a dull sound. I pulled the red-black blood into the hypodermic. Three cubic centimeters… five cubic centimeters… His face became paler. Before, he'd been moaning; now he could not even moan. His throat was making a tiny rasping sound like an insect. With resentment and anger in his eyes. He stared at me without even blinking. But that did not matter. I obtained a blood sample of ten cubic centimeters. For people in laboratory work, this is ecstasy, and one's calling to his profession. Showing compassion for a person's death pains was of no value to me. At the lab,

I processed the blood sample quickly and then went back to look into the cell. His face occasionally twitched. His breath became shallower, and he went into his death throes. The other four men in the cell, who had the same fate waiting for them, could not contain their anger. They took water and poured it into the mouth of the dead man. This way, an irreplaceable life is trifled with to take the place of a guinea pig, and the result is one sheet of graph paper. Four or five soldiers, with drawn guns, opened the door to the cell. It made a heavy sound. They dragged the dead man out into the corridor and loaded him onto a hand cart. The other four men, knowing what their fate would be tomorrow, could not hold down the anger in their eyes as they watched their dead companion leave. The hand cart disappeared in the direction of the dissection room with the tall chimney looming above."[24]

As requested by the Command of the Japanese Air Force, Unit 731 also housed a pressure chamber to test the endurance of human organs at high altitudes. In this chamber, men died painful deaths.[25]

Many sacrificed their lives for scientific advancement and it was well known in the Japanese scientific community that humans were used as test subjects for their scientific papers. In fact, some scientific papers

---

[24] Gold, Hal, *Unit 731 Testimony*, p. 41-44.
[25] *Khabarovsk Trial Opening*.

from Unit 731 researchers referred to their subjects as "Manchurian monkeys", "monkeys", "Taiwan monkey", and "Formosan monkey". It was an open secret in the Japanese medical society that they were using humans as experimental subjects.[26]

---

[26] Tsuneishi, "Research Guarded by Military Secrecy," p. 89.

Chapter 6

Vivisection

Ethics did not exist in Ishii's Network. Everything was done efficiently in the name of science. Vivisection was conducted on human beings to better observe first-hand how diseases affected each organ once a human dies; the putrefactive bacteria could set in and destroy the result of a good experiment. Even though the logs held in Unit 731's inner prison were in shackles, their health and nutrients were monitored since good health could guarantee the best scientific results for their experiments. An Ishii technician described what the maruta were served. "Only at noon was there a small amount of soybean mixed in... Full consideration was given to the nutrient value of supplements, and pork was served in a different menu almost every day."[27]

Every laboratory at Pingfan had a large bulletin board with technicians recording data such as "Spe-

---

[27] Tsuneishi, *The Germ Warfare Unit that Disappeared*, p. 67-68.

cific date; 3 maruta, numbers so and so, were given injections of so-and-so, x cc; we need x number of hearts or x number of livers, etc."[28] In a testimony given on December 28 by witness Furuichi during the Khabarovsk Trial, he described how "a Russian woman was infected with syphilis to allow the scientists to find out how to prevent the spread of the disease.[29] Many babies were born to women who had been captured and become experimental subjects. Some women were kidnapped while pregnant; others became pregnant after forced sex acts in the prisons, enabling researchers to study the transmission of venereal disease.[30]

According to testimony given by a technician, Ogawa Fukumatsu, in a video interview years after the war, he stated, "I participated in vivisections. I did them every day. I cannot remember the amount of people dissected. At first, I refused to do it. But then, they would not allow me to eat because it was an order; gradually I changed."

Masakuni Kuri testified as well. "I did vivisection at the time. Experiments were conducted on a Chinese woman with syphilis. Because she was alive, the blood poured out like water from a tap."

---

[28] Dong, "Kwantung Army 731".
[29] *Khabarovsk Trial*, p. 286.
[30] Hal Gold, *Unit 731 Testimony*, p. 45.

Chapter 6: Vivisection

Ken Yuasa, a former doctor of Unit 731 stated in a video interview, "In the room, there were over 10 surgeons waiting for practice. A nurse about 20 years old stood beside the operating table. It was not quiet. Everyone was laughing and joking just as usual. Then the experiment started. This time it was a Chinese man. I don't know how he was captured. We did not care whether he was innocent or not. Someone pushed him hard and he cried while kneeling on the ground struggling backward. I also pushed him really hard. Later he seemed exhausted and gave up hope. The nurse said to him in Chinese that he could sleep and that the anesthetic would prevent any pain. He walked toward the operating table and laid on it. The vivisectionist wasn't very skilled. He cut a big opening on the belly, poured out the intestine, caught them and connected them. I stood aside to direct. The man was still in front of me as if he was dead. Altogether, six experiments were done on him including one where his arm was amputated. Almost one and a half hour later, the operation ended and he was dead."

Ishii's network had recruited Youth Corps members for vivisection as well. Since wartime Japan fostered a sense of nationalism in everyone, children were encouraged to report to the school principal any anti-war sentiments of their parents. The police were then to investigate the parents. Many children were also encouraged by their teachers to enter the Youth Corps. Some Youth Corps members were just 15-17 when they started working at Unit 731. They went through rigorous training in biology, foreign languages, math, and bacteriology.[31] Most of them became assistants to researchers at Unit 731 where their main duty was to remove organs from a human body during a vivisection. According to former Youth Class Member at Unit 731, Shinotsuka Ryu, "At first I was terrified, my legs were shaking, they told me I could use the longest brush. After the vivisection, the victims were unrecognizable. I was ordered to put their organs into containers. We used them to cultivate bacteria."[32]

It was estimated that about 3000 people went through human experimentations in Unit 731 from 1940 to 1945. However, that is considered a low estimate since the capacity of the prisons was a lot higher and some victims did not survive for more than an average of two weeks.

The Reports of A, G, and Q by Shozo Kondo Toshu are examples of such vivisection experiments. Each report was 350 to 800 pages long and represented only a small fraction of the methods used to turn

---

[31] Ibid, p. 61.
[32] *New China TV*, "Japanese World War II Veterans Recall Horrors of Unit 731".

human lives into data points for scientific papers. The author's reports sounded very removed from the human lives that were lost through his research.

Report "A" described how victims react to anthrax. About 30 subjects were used in that study and the reports of different effects of anthrax was very objective. There were no notes on the subjects' names, gender, ethnicities, or identification of any kind. However, the age range of the subjects averaged from 20s to 30s. Although there was no definite gender listed for the subjects, the presence of testicles examined as an organ showed all the test subjects were males. All subjects infected with anthrax in the study survived around 2-4 days.

Descriptions of the vivisections and procedures included the use of X-Rays before vivisections. The consistent mention of "X-rays during clinical tests" suggests that most, if not all, of the subjects were examined closely while infected with anthrax until they died. The "A" Report lacks any specific descriptions of vivisection or autopsy procedures, but shows clearly how the scientists converted the test subjects' lives into a report of test subject data.

From detailed reported notes on the results of the disease, the effects of the "A" pathogen, Anthrax, included:

- General parenchymatous degeneration (swelling and degeneration of cells and cell membranes).
- **Tonsils**: Catarrh (excessive discharge of mucus from inflammation of mucous membrane, causing congestion), superficial ulcers (sores on the upper layer of organ tissue), intense tonsillitis with extensive effects (listed below).
- **Intense Tonsillitis**: Inflammation of the tonsils, causing difficulty swallowing and sore throat. This then caused:
- **Peribronchitis**: Inflammation and swelling of tissue around the bronchi, the airways to the lungs, congestion causing difficulty breathing and coughing (as well as general bronchitis).
- **Mediastinitis**: Inflammation and swelling of the mediastinum, the chest cavity that contains the heart, the esophagus, the thyroid, and many other organs in the chest and throat.
- **Hemorrhagic exudation in the peribronchial and mediastinal tissues**: Secretion and leaking of blood in the chest cavity and the tissue surrounding the bronchi, the part of the lungs that expand and compress when taking in air.
- **Skin**: Cutaneous ulcers (skin ulcers), perifocal phlegmons (inflamed soft tissue under skin).
- **Abdomen**: Intense hemorrhagic exudative changes in small and large intestines (secretion of blood out of blood vessels), intense hemor-

rhagic ascites in the abdomen (massive excess buildup of blood causing large abdominal swelling and stomach bulging), leukocyte congestion of the small and large intestines (cell fluid congesting intestines), lymphadenitis with hemorrhaging (swelling and bleeding of the lymph nodes).

- **Lungs**: Alveolitis (tissue development in the lungs resulting in difficulty breathing), bacterial dissemination (general infection of a virus leading to cell decay), tuberculosis, atelectasis (collapse and loss of lung volume, causes respiratory failure).
- **Heart**: Intense degeneration of the heart (general breakdown of all parts of the heart from literally falling apart), interstitial edema of the heart (swelling in the fluid-filled space of muscular and cell walls).
- **Liver**: Hepatitis (inflammation of the liver), intense hepatitis serosa in the liver (scab scarring and degeneration of the liver), general hemorrhaging in the liver (internal bleeding), multiple miliary necrosis (rashes and wounds that cause mass cell death), fat degeneration.
- **Stomach**: Mucus catarrh (excessive buildup of mucus from the inflammation of the mucous membrane), congestion in mucous and sub-mucous tissues (causing difficulty digesting food).

- **Kidney**: Glomerulo/nephrosis in the kidney (degeneration of nerve endings and intersecting blood vessels leading to kidney failure), vacuolar degeneration of epitheliums in kidney (degeneration of the outer lining of the kidney), considerable interstitial edema (swelling in the fluid-filled space of muscular and cell walls).
- **Pancreas**: Intense parenchymatous degeneration (cell swelling and increase in cellular water leading to cell congestion and death), fluid congestion, general cell degeneration.
- **Spleen**: Spleenitis infections in spleen (inflammation of the spleen, leading in slowed function).
- **Brain**: Diffuse hemorrhages in general suprarenal and cortical tissues (bleeding in the outer layer of the brain's tissue and the brain's adrenal gland), intense suprarenal degeneration (breakdown of a hormonal gland inside the brain), general congestion of cerebellum.
- **Thyroid**: Floccular collapse (degeneration and collapse of thyroid).
- **Testicles**: Atrophia Testes (for male subjects, shrinking and ceasing function of testicles).

The "G" Report by Shozo Kondo Toshu concerned the biological effects of glanders. Similar to the "A"

Report, the number of subjects examined was about 21, based on the amount of actual detailed reports. All subjects had differing survival times, though most fell under a two-month span. From infection onset, some survived for 4-12 days, while others survived for 15-25 days, with the remaining few surviving for 25 days to a month. One subject lasted 3 months before death. There were no notes on the subjects' names, gender, ethnicity, or any kind of identification aside from their age. The age range of the subjects averaged between mid-20s and mid-30s. Although there were no definite genders listed for the subjects, the presence of testicles being an examined organ suggests that all of the subjects were male.

In the report, there were descriptions of vivisection and procedures such that X-Rays used before vivisections. The consistent mention of "X-rays during clinical tests" suggests that most, if not all, of the subjects were examined closely while infected with glanders. Vivisections examined all organs that could possibly be affected and there was a detailed report for every organ of every subject. The procedures in The "G" Report were almost certainly vivisections. This was due to there being multiple points in which the author referred to information about the disease's progression that could only be attained by having dissected the subject before they died—days or weeks before the disease evolved to its final, lethal, stage. However, similar to the "A" Report, this report lacks any specific description of the vivisection procedures as it is more of a report of the results. On page 109 of *The Report of "G,"* the author states, "I cannot explain 'the methods of infection and clinical symptoms' in detail, while I have not received these records." This shows that the author, though present at the vivisections of the subjects (in order to even create the report), did not oversee the entire process of infecting and monitoring the subjects. This explains why there is so little information on the details or circumstances of the vivisections; the author was most likely not present for some portion of the experiment likely performed by a low level technician.

From detailed notes on the reported results of the disease, the effects of glanders disease, include:

- **Heart**: Interstitial edema in the subendocardial tissues (swelling in the fluid-filled space of muscular walls of the heart which contain nerves and impulse-conducting system that allows it to beat), miliary glanders-knots (scabs and rashes in the inner tissues of the heart, some of which inhibit the flow of blood in the heart through swelling), degeneration in the cartilage of the heart (weakening and deterioration of the heart, reducing its ability to circulate blood), Rheumatoid-knots formations (firm lumps of skin, possibly causing clotting and decreased blood flow in the heart).

- **Lungs:** Metastatic endarteritis (development of cancer cells in the inner linings of arteries or veins in the lungs, causing inflammation), acinolobular pneumonia (pneumonia focused at the very ends of the tiny airways inside the lungs, near the alveoli), reactive pleuritis (inflammation of the lining of the lungs, causing sharp chest pain and shallow breathing), miliary glanders-knots (scabs and rashes in the inner tissues of the lungs, causing more pain and possible internal bleeding), increase in alveolar epitheliums (large cells that are responsible for the oxygen and carbon dioxide exchange in the lungs).

- **Liver:** Exudation in disse space from hepatitis serosa (fluid leaking through blood plasma, the liquid that holds blood cells together, from scab scarring and degeneration of the liver), proliferated miliary glanders-knots (multiplying scabs and rashes in the inner tissues of the liver, damaging blood cells and reducing blood circulation throughout the liver), hyperplasia of Kupfer's cells (enlargement of the liver from a higher rate of cell production, resulting from the initial stage of cancer).

- **Kidney**: Glomerulo-nephrosis (degeneration of nerve endings and intersecting blood vessels leading to kidney failure), edema (swelling of the kidney), miliary glanders-knots (scabs, rashes and bumps inside the kidney causing congestion and loss of circulation), hyperplasia of reticulum cells (enlargement and increase of production of cells in the kidney, resulting from the initial stage of cancer), giant cell formation (resulting from hyperplasia, causes lack of cell movement and loss of function

- **Intestines**: Submucous congestion (congestion of mucous production, causing difficulty digesting food), miliary glanders-knots (scabs, rashes, and bumps in the inner tissues of the intestines, causing congested blood flow and slowdown of general intestines function), hyperplasia of reticulum cells (enlargement and increase of production of cells, resulting from the initial stage of cancer, leading to the formation of tumors).

- **Suprarenal Gland**: Epinephritis serosa (scab scarring and degeneration of the suprarenal gland, partially causing inflammation), hemorrhages (internal bleeding of the suprarenal gland), round cell accumulation (highly concentrated and aggressive malignant tumors, causing cancer).

- **Pancreas**: General degeneration (general breakdown of all parts of the pancreas, leading to cease of function), perivascular edema (inflammation of the blood vessels, congesting blood flow), hemorrhages (internal bleed of the pancreas), serous apoplexy (cease of function due to cerebral hemorrhaging and stroke, with excess fluid surrounding the areas affected), round cell accumulation (highly concentrated and aggressive malignant tumors, causing cancer).
- **Pituitary Body**: Pituitaritis serosa (inflammation of the outer layer of the pituitary body that contains serous, lubricating fluid), hemorrhaging (internal bleeding of the brain).
- **Meninges**: Congestion (decreased blood flow in the membranes that line the skull and the brain), hemorrhaging (internal bleeding of the brain).
- **Muscles**: General abscess (swollen pockets inside various muscles around the body, containing puss), hyperplasia in myoblast, histiocyte, and fibroblast cells (increase in the production of cells throughout the body, surrounding the muscles, leading to cancer).
- **Spleen**: Angio-folliculitis (inflammation of hair follicles leading to hair loss and scarring

due to sweat gland congestion from spleen dysfunction), hemmorhagic-exudativa (flow of mass cell fluid out of an internal wound and bleeding), hyperplasia (increase in the production of cells in the spleen, leading to cancer).
- **Testicles**: Atrophia Testes (for male subjects, shrinking and ceasing function of the testicles).

The "Q" report, also by Shozo Kondo, is a study of the effects of bubonic plague on humans. The number of subjects in the study was 57, ranging in age from toddlers to 80 year olds with mixed genders. This study described spreading the plague by dispersing fleas among the local population in June of 1940 in Noan and Shinkyo (currently Changchun). Seven of the plague victims were Japanese residing in Shinkyo at the time. The report also states that "Shinkyo" could not be contaminated for some time, though the language used is highly unclear on whether or not contaminating the city with the plague was a desired objective. The city was eventually contaminated by plague epidemics emerging in the "Noan-region" and that eventually spread to "Shinkyo" due to the lack of immunity developed by townspeople. (Due to this, we may assume "Noan" is somewhere near "Shinkyo" or Changchun).

The length of subjects' survival time was fairly consistent in the report, ranging from 2-5 days, with only three surviving 12, 18, and 21 days. Additionally, the range of what the subjects were infected with varied from Glandular, Cutaneous, or Septicemic Plague, but most of the subjects were infected with the Glandular Plague. The report was most likely done by autopsy instead of vivisection since they probably collected the dead from their biological weapons attack at the time.

Detailed notes on the effects of the disease reported the effects of the bubonic plague and include:

- **Heart**: Intense degeneration and atrophy (general breakdown and weakening of all parts of the heart, causing cease of function and heart failure), congestion and bacterial buildup in capillaries (buildup of diseased material in the many small veins throughout the heart, halting blood flow throughout the heart), congestion of tissue around the aorta (diseased material buildup around the main vein of the heart, causing radically decreased blood flow and possible heart attacks or strokes), some round cell accumulation (highly concentrated and aggressive malignant tumors, causing cancer)
- **Tonsil**: Submucous congestion (swelling in the lower layer of cells of the mucous membrane due to problems in blood flow, causing further

blood flow congestion and leakage of blood cells), bacterial buildup in capillaries (congestion in the small veins throughout the tonsils, slowing blood flow), edema (swelling of the tonsils, causing difficulty breathing, speaking, or swallowing)

- **Pharynx**: Intense congestion (causing extreme difficulty eating, swallowing, breathing, or speaking), catarrh (excessive discharge of mucus from inflammation of mucous membrane, causing congestion)
- **Epiglottis**: Intense congestion and edema (swelling and bacterial buildup on the leaf-shaped flap that stops food from entering the windpipe/lungs, causing extreme difficulty breathing, swallowing, or speaking)
- **Lungs**: Bronchitis catarrhalis gravis (inflammation and buildup of bacterial mucus, causing painful coughing, difficulty breathing and swallowing, fatigue, as well as muscular weakening of the lungs themselves, which then causes extreme cases of the former symptoms, along with intense shortness of breath, slowed movement, and eventual cease of lung function), lobular edema (swelling in the lungs, causing difficulty breathing and processing oxygen) pneumonic consolidation (the replacement of air with intrusive fluid in consoli-

dated lung tissue, causing extreme difficulty breathing and processing air), bacterial masses in capillaries (congestion of blood vessels, causing failure of blood circulation)
- **Liver**: Intense hepatitis serosa (degenerative scabbing and scarring of the liver, causing extreme liver weakness), multiple miliary necrosis (sudden rashes and wounds, causing mass cell death)
- **Stomach**: Atrophy (wasting away of the stomach, causing extreme weakness and inefficiency of digestion, eventually leading to failure), hemorrhaging (internal bleeding of the stomach)
- **Large Intestine**: Catarrh (excessive discharge of mucus from inflammation of mucous membrane, causing congestion and difficulty digesting)
- **Kidney**: Glomerulo-nephrosis (degeneration of nerve endings and intersecting blood vessels leading to kidney failure), polar edema (inflammation and swelling in specific, localized parts of the kidney)
- **Spleen**: Angio-folliculitis (inflammation of hair follicles leading to hair loss and scarring due to sweat gland congestion from spleen dysfunction), Fasciculitis (most likely fasciitis, which is the inflammation of the facia, and when that tissue is inflamed, it can cut off

blood supply in the blood vessels, which causes the tissue to not receive oxygen and die)

- **Pancreas:** Intense parenchymatous degeneration (cell swelling and increase in cellular water leading to cell congestion and death), bacterial masses in capillaries (congestion of blood vessels, causing failure of blood flow)
- **Suprarenal Gland:** Autolysis (self-digestion, destruction of cells from their own enzymes).
- **Thyroid:** Follicular collapse (collapse and loss of form of the thyroid, ceasing delivery of hormones)
- **Lymph-nodes:** Lymphadenitis haemorrhagica totalis (inflammation of the lymph nodes to the point of extreme bleeding from its entirety)
- **Skin:** Phlegmons with cutaneous ulcers (mass inflamed skin accompanied by ulcers and skin sores, causing loss of upper skin layer)

Researching and understanding how germs work was important to Unit 731 since the first division was engaged in breeding plague and cholera germs, gas gangrene, anthrax, typhoid, paratyphoid fever, and other diseases for their use in bacteriological warfare.

Chapter 7

Anta Testing Grounds

The delivery of weapons needed to be proven scientifically and it was the duty of the 2nd division with airplane bombers to handle tests of bacteriological weapons on a proving ground as well as under battle conditions for the mass extermination of human beings. Because the Anta Testing Grounds were only 146 kilometers north of Harbin, Ishii used a light aircraft for the short flight if the only people traveling were him and his aide.[33]

According to Kawashima during an interrogation of the Khabarovsk Trial on December 25, "In the summer of 1941, the Chief of the detachment, Ishii, called a conference of all the chiefs of divisions and informed us that an instruction had been received from the Chief of Staff of the Japanese Army, the substance of which was as follows: Detachment 731 had done good work in preparation for bacteriologi-

---

[33] Harris, Sheldon, *Factories of Death*, p. 58.

cal warfare and, in particular, in the breeding of plague fleas on a mass scale. Plague fleas were of great operational and strategical interest, and it was therefore instructed that research work in this field should be intensified. The Chief of the detachment pointed out that one of the detachment's weakest points was its inadequate facilities for breeding fleas on a mass scale, and that "all attention must be focused on the mass production of fleas."

The 2nd division controlled an aircraft unit with specially equipped planes near the Anta testing grounds as well as a section that engaged in the cultivation and breeding of parasites intended to cause plague epidemics. In a testimony by Kawashima during the Khabarovsk Trial, he stated, "… With the available equipment and its rate of output, the Production Division… could manufacture as much as 300 kilograms of plague bacteria monthly, or 800 to 900 kilograms of typhoid germs". This was also verified by another accused in the Khabarovsk Trial, "… The monthly output of the germ producing division could be raised… if all its equipment were fully operated, to about 300 kilograms of plague bacteria."[34]

The wholesale breeding of fleas using rodents such as mice and rats was also utilized as a line of defense as a type of bacteriological weapon, not only

---

[34] *Khabarovsk Trial*, Vol. 4, p. 286.

for the personnel bacteriological unit's personnel, but also by special squads detailed from line troops of the Kwantung Army. In Branch 543 of Ishii's Network in Hailar, there were about 13,000 rats in the summer of 1945.[35] In fact, there were multiple branches of Unit 731 close to the Mongolian People's Republic and the Soviet Union in locations such as Sunyu, Hailar, Linkow, and Hailin.

The Chief of Branch 673 of Unit 731 was located in the town of Sunyu, and the Chief of the Training Division of the detachment, Nishi Toshihide, testified that, From January 1943 to July 1944, and then from June to August 1945, I was in charge of Branch 673 of Detachment 731 in the town of Sunye, which was engage in breeding white rats, mice, and guinea pigs, in catching field rodents and in breeding fleas… In particular, the breeding and catching of rodents and the breeding of fleas to be sent to Detachment 731 were intensified, since the spreading of plague germs by scattering plague-infected fleas was regarded as the most effective means of bacteriological warfare." It was to be kept an extreme secret as he continued, "On August 11-12, 1945, owing to the advance of the Soviet Army, and with the object of concealing the fact that weapons for conducting bacteriological warfare had been manufactured

---

[35] Ibid, Vol. 2, p. 239.

in the Japanese Kwantung Army and that Branch 673 of Detachment 731 under my command had been involved in these criminal activities, on my orders all the branch's service premises and living quarters, equipment, materials, and documents were destroyed by fire, and for the same purpose, on my orders, on August 14, 1945, poison in the shape of potassium cyanide was issued to the entire personnel (120 men) to be taken by them to commit suicide in the event of the danger arising of their being captured by the Soviet forces."

They also designed special weapons for germs dissemination: sprayers in the form of fountain pens and walking sticks, porcelain aerial bombs, and others for sabotage missions. Unit 731's and Unit 100's production facilities were designed for an active prosecution of bacteriological warfare.[36] According to the Japanese Imperial Army's plans, specially equipped aircraft, specially trained army units, and sabotage squads were to disseminate large quantities of lethal germs of plague, cholera, typhoid, glanders, anthrax, and other severe infectious diseases along the enemy's territory targeting soil, water sources, wells, crops, and cattle, and every possible front. The purpose was to cause epidemics among the civilian population that would result in millions of painful deaths.

---

[36] Ibid, Vol. 9, p. 155.

Chapter 7: Anta Testing Grounds

At the Anta testing grounds, to test the biological weapons the unit was developing, were usually bacteria shells filled with plague and anthrax germs, gas gangrene, and other disease producing substances were exploded in direct proximity to victims tied to stakes. This was to observe firsthand the action of various bacteria as ammunition. In testimony by Kawashima during the Khabarovsk Trial on December 25, he stated, "Very soon after my appointment to Detachment 731, that is, in the summer of 1941, experiments were performed at Anta Station on the use of the Ishii porcelain bomb charged with plague fleas. The site used for the tests was very carefully guarded and no one was allowed to pass through. Special sentry posts were stationed around it, which guarded the place so that no unauthorized person could enter it. The persons used for these experiments, fifteen in number, were brought from the detachment's inner prison to the experimental ground and tied to stakes which had been driven into the ground for the purpose. Flags and smoke signals were used to guide the planes and enable them to find the proving ground easily. A special plane took off from Pingfan Station, and when it was over the site it dropped about two dozen bombs, which burst at about 100 or 200 meters from the ground, releasing the plague fleas with which they were charged. The plague fleas were dispersed all over the territory. A long interval was allowed to pass after the bombs had been dropped in order the fleas might spread and infect the test subjects. These people were then disinfected and taken back by plane to the inner prison at Pingfan Station, where observation was established over them to ascertain whether they had been infected with plague."[37]

Another employee of Unit 731, Karasawa stated, "… I personally was present on two occasions at the Anta proving ground when the action of bacteria was tested on human beings under field conditions. The first time I was there towards the end of 1943. Some ten persons were brought to the proving ground, were tied to stakes which had been previously driven into the ground five meters apart, and a fragmentation bomb was exploded by electric current about 50 meters away from them. A number of those tested were injured by bomb splinters and simultaneously, as I afterwards learned, infected with anthrax, since the bomb was charged with these bacteria. The second time I visited the proving ground was in the spring of 1944; about ten people were brought there, and, as on the first occasion, tied to stakes. A cylinder filled with plague germs was then exploded at a distance of roughly ten meters from the test subjects."[38]

---

[37] Ibid, *December 25th*.
[38] Ibid, Vol 4, p. 42.

Further testimony by Nishi Toshihide verified the criminal experiments at the Anta proving ground, "... In January 1945, in my presence, Lieutenant Colonel Ikrai, Chief of the 2nd Division of Detachment 731, and Futaki, a research official of this division, performed an experiment at the detachment's proving ground near Anta Station, infecting ten Chinese war prisoners with gas gangrene. The ten Chinese prisoners were tied to stakes from 10 to 20 meters apart, and a bomb was then exploded by electricity. All ten were injured by shrapnel contaminated with gas gangrene germs and within a week they all died in severe torment."[39]

According to witness Fukuzumi Mitsuyoshi, they were engaged in, "... Research in methods for the mass employment of bacteria was conducted by means of experiments on special proving grounds, special apparatus and aircraft being used. Large scale experiments of this kind were called 'maneuvers.' Such 'maneuvers' were held in September 1944 at Anta Station... The experiments were made on 300 cattle and sheep. This experiment showed good results, as all the animals were infected and died. Representatives of the Headquarters of the Kwantung Army arrived by plane to witness these maneuvers."[40]

---

[39] Ibid, Vol. 7, p. 113.
[40] Ibid, Vol. 13, p. 49.

Experiments at Anta Station, enabled Unit 731 to better engage in biological warfare. For example, as Kawashima testified in the Khabarovsk Trial about an incident in the Nimpo area in 1940, "General Ishii showed me a Chinese medical journal in which the causes of an outbreak of plague in the Nimpo area in 1940 were discussed. After showing me the journal he told me that a Detachment 731 expedition had dropped plague fleas from an airplane in the Nimpo area, and that this was the cause of the outbreak of the epidemic." The Nimpo area outbreak was well documented by a student named Kaneko Junichi in a dissertation for his PhD at Tokyo University. In his chart of the effectiveness of six types of biological warfare operated by Unit 731 from June 1940 to August 1942, it was very clearly stated that the plague outbreak peaked by day 10.[41] Besides bubonic plague, anthrax and glanders were also used. Villagers in the region suffered from rotten leg diseases for many years after the war.[42]

Another incident described, "... in the summer of 1941. One day, Colonel Oota, Chief of the 2nd Division, told me that he was going to Central China and said goodbye to me. Sometime after his return he

---

[41] 国立国会図書館, Junichi Kaneko 金子順一, PX Effects of Plague Weapon, 1944.

[42] *Seeking Justice for Biological Warfare Victims of Unit 731: Evidence Collected*, p. 54.

told me that plague fleas had been dropped from aircraft on the Chinese in the area of the city of Changteh, near Lake Tung Ting Hu, in Central China. This, in effect, was a bacteriological attack, which was the term he used. After this, Colonel Oota made a report to Chief of Detachment 731 Ishii, at which I was present, to the effect that the Detachment 731 expedition had dropped plague fleas from an airplane in the Changteh area, and that an outbreak of plague epidemic had resulted, a number of persons being stricken with the disease, but how many, I do not know." The incident described by Kawashima was done by an expedition of 40-50 men who sprayed plague fleas from aircraft at a high altitude.[43]

From their research, they came out with the designs of these bacteriological bombs.

---

[43] *Khabarovsk Trial, December 25th Examination of Kawashima.*

"Type 50 Uji Bombs—The 25 kg, 10 liters, Type 50 Uji bomb was an improved model of the Uji series of bombs. The nose contained an impact, delay fuse and a bursting tube with TNT. A time fuze in the tail set off the 4 meters of primacord exploding the bomb at a height of 200 to 300 meters. In case the tail fuze and the primacord failed to function, explosion of the bomb with dispersion of the contents was insured upon impact by the explosive train in the nose. Approximately 500 rounds of this model were manufactured in 1940 and 1941, and extensive field trials were conducted during the period 1940 to 1942. The bomb was tested by static explosion and drop tests from aircraft. For the initial tests the bomb was filled with dye solution and suspensions of nonpathogenic organisms. Later trials were conducted using a suspension of anthrax spores as the payload. The suspension had a concentration of 50 to 100 milligrams of spores per cubic centimeter of liquid."

Chapter 7: Anta Testing Grounds

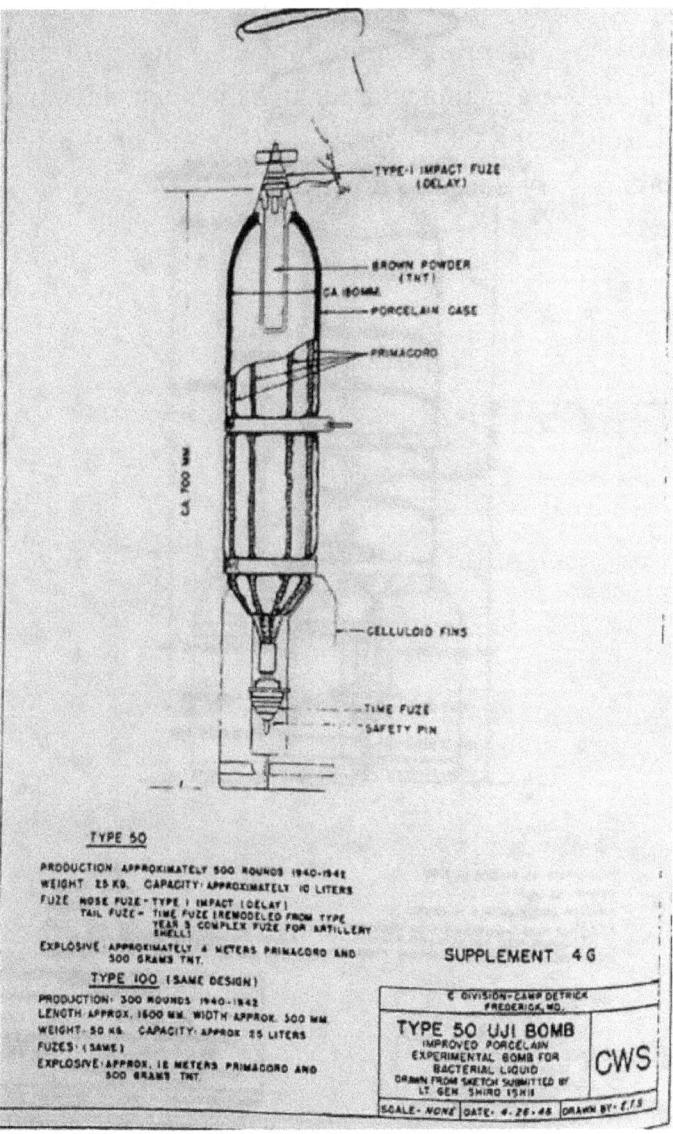

"Ga Bomb—The 35 kg Ga bomb was an experimental glass case model of the Old Type Uji Bomb. Spiral instead of longitudinal grooves contained the explosive of primacord. Only 20 rounds of this model were manufactured. It had much the same defects as the Old Type Uji bomb and after a few preliminary trials was discarded."

Chapter 7: Anta Testing Grounds

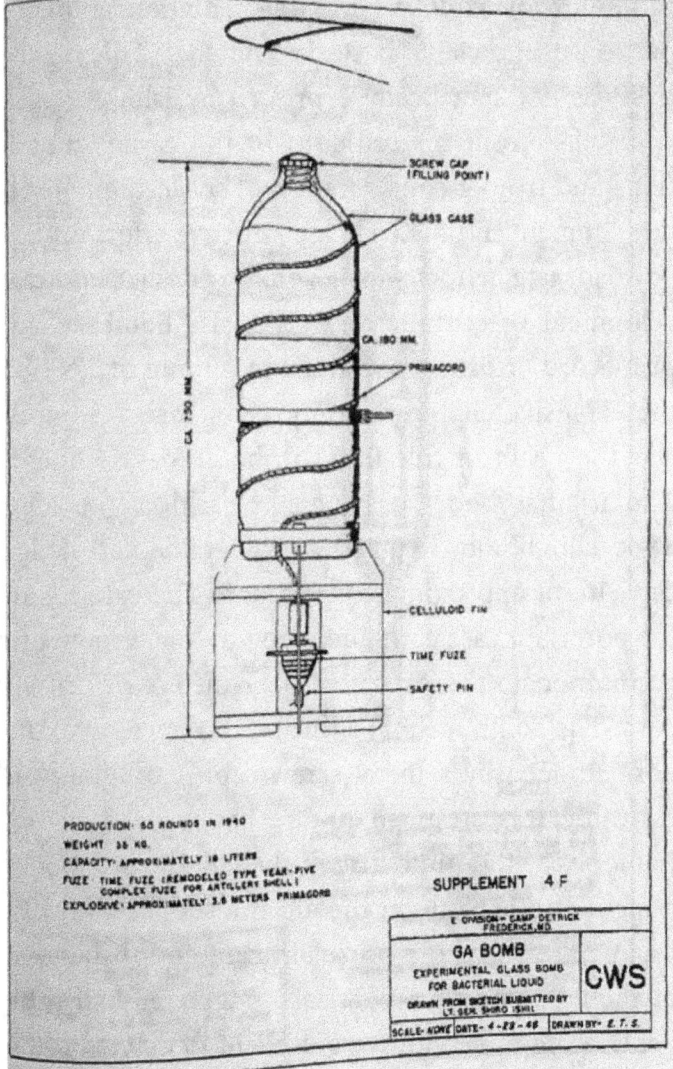

"Old Type Uji Bomb—By 1938, the trend in Japanese munition development was towards bombs of simpler design, greater capacity, and requiring a minimum of explosive for fragmentation and dispersion of the viable bacterial contents. This objective was not specifically expressed by Ishii but it is concluded from his criticism of the earlier munitions and from a consideration of succeeding bomb development. From steel case structive effect on the payload, later effort was devoted to design and development of ceramic and glass case bombs using primacord or primacord and a minimum of TNT as the explosive charge. The porcelain case Uji bomb was the result of this trend in bomb development. The original model, designated by Ishii as the "Old Type Uji" bomb, weighed 25 kilograms and had a capacity of approximately 10 liters. The exterior of the porcelain case contained longitudinal grooves to accommodate the explosive of 4 meters of primacord. The bomb was filled through an opening in the nose stopped by a metal screw cap. A celluloid fin assembly was strapped to the base of the bomb. Equipped with a time fuse in the tail, the bomb was designed to explode in the air at a set altitude with fragmentation of the porcelain case and dispersion of the contents. The porcelain fragments had little penetrating force, but were difficult to detect on the ground. The bomb was tested in 1938 on a field layout such as for the I, Ro, and Ha bombs using dye or starch solutions and suspensions of nonpathogenic organisms. In static tests, exploded at a height of 15 meters, an area of dispersion 20-30 by 500-600 meters resulted with a wind velocity of 5 meters per second. In drop tests, areas of dispersion 20-30 by 500-700 meters resulted when the bomb was exploded at altitudes of 200 to 300 meters. Particle size of the disseminated liquid contents ranged from 'droplets the size of raindrops, and larger drops due to aggregation, to particles 50 microns in diameter.'"

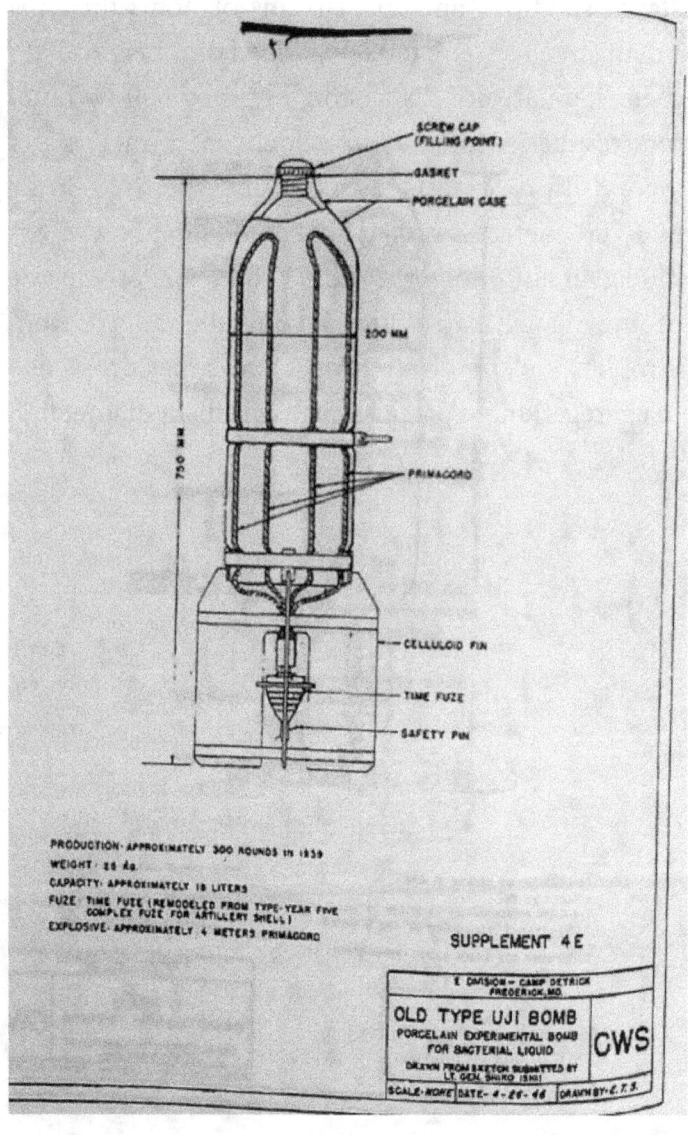

"U Bomb—The 30kg U bomb was designed to spray liquids by means of compressed air at a predetermined altitude. The bomb had a detachable nose covering a spray head. It was equipped with an impact nose fuze, a delay tail fuze and a self-timing tail mechanism which operated upon release from the airplane. Action of the self-timer allowed the central burster tube to move forward separating the detachable nose from the spray head. The forward motion of the central burster tube also caused release of the compressed air with spraying of the bomb itself exploded. Only 20 rounds of this bomb were manufactured, Ishii said, and no field experiments were conducted aside from tests to determine bomb function. Because of leakage of the contents, defective fuzes, inaccurate timing mechanism, and because of its complicated structure the U bomb was not considered worthy of further development and was discarded."

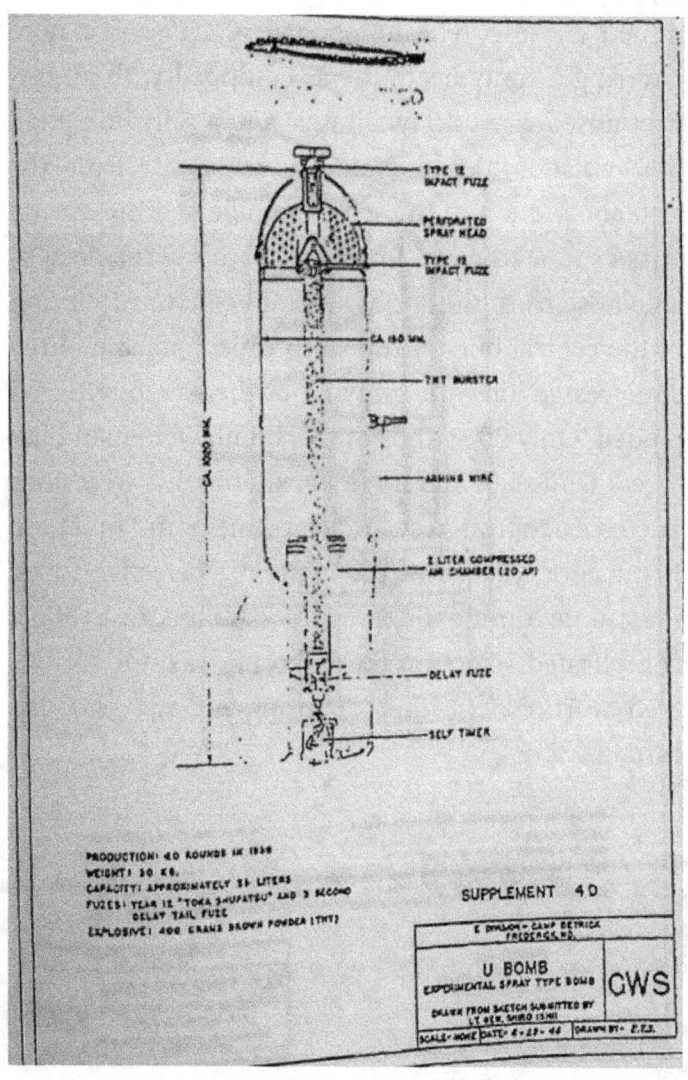

Chapter 7: Anta Testing Grounds

"Ni Bomb—The 50 kg Ni bomb was of the same general design as the Ha bomb. The bomb body was about 100 millimeters longer, and it had a payload capacity of 1 liter. The explosive charge, however, was only 50 percent of that used in the Ha bomb. Due to the smaller explosive charge, bacterial survival was greater, but the penetrating force of the bomb fragments and area of dispersion was not as great. Results from tests of the bomb in 1939 were considered to be 'rather good,' and the bomb was deemed worthy of further development."

"Ha Bomb—The 40 kg Ha bomb was a fragmentation bomb designed for destructive effect by projection of bomb fragments and shrapnel contaminated with anthrax spores. The bomb was double walled, having a central burster tube surrounded by an iron fragmentation wall 10 millimeters in thickness, and a payload chamber between the wall and the steel bomb case. The payload chamber was of 700 cubic centimeters capacity and contained about 1,500 steel pellets to augment the destructive effects of the bomb fragments. The payload chamber and the steel pellets were coated with a bakelite varnish to prevent corrosion. Armed with nose and tail impact fuses and containing 3 kilograms of TNT in the nose and tail compartments and central burster tube, the bomb exploded upon impact scattering bomb fragments, shrapnel and anthrax spores at high velocity in a horizontal direction.

Field trials of the Ha bomb were made during 1938 and 1939. Dye solutions and organisms were used as fill for the static tests. Size, distribution and penetrating power of the bomb fragments and shrapnel were determined by using a grid consisting of upright board targets arranged in concentric circles from the point of bomb burst. Test animals were distributed in like pattern. In winter, fragmentation distribution was determined by recovery of particles from the frozen, icy ground. Fragments and shrapnel were projected for distances of 400 to 500 meters with a density of about one fragment or shrapnel per square meter within a radius of 50 meters. Bomb fragments and shrapnel were recovered and examined for viability of attached organisms. Drop trials were made from aircraft for the purpose of deterring bomb function and percentage of duds.

Additional fragmentation studies were made by burying the bomb in sand to a depth of 5 meters. The bomb was then exploded electrically and the sand screened to estimate the size of the resulting fragments. Approximately 10 percent of the recovered fragments weighed from 1 to 3 grams, 20 percent from 3 to 5 grams, 25 percent from 5 to 10 grams, 40 percent from 10 to 15 grams, and 5 percent were over 15 grams.

The Ha bomb had several defects. It was considered too complex for mass production. The thin bomb case was soldered to the head and tail sections and would not withstand the shock of handling and transportation. Leakage of the bacterial contents often occurred, with danger of infection to the bomb handlers. Suspension of the bomb in aircraft was difficult because the shape of the bomb varied from that of standard aircraft bombs. The heavy explosive charge destroyed 40 to 65 percent of the organisms. Regardless of its defects the Ha bomb was considered promising. Ishii believed that, with correction of the defects and further development by bomb experts, the Ha bomb could be made into an efficient munition."

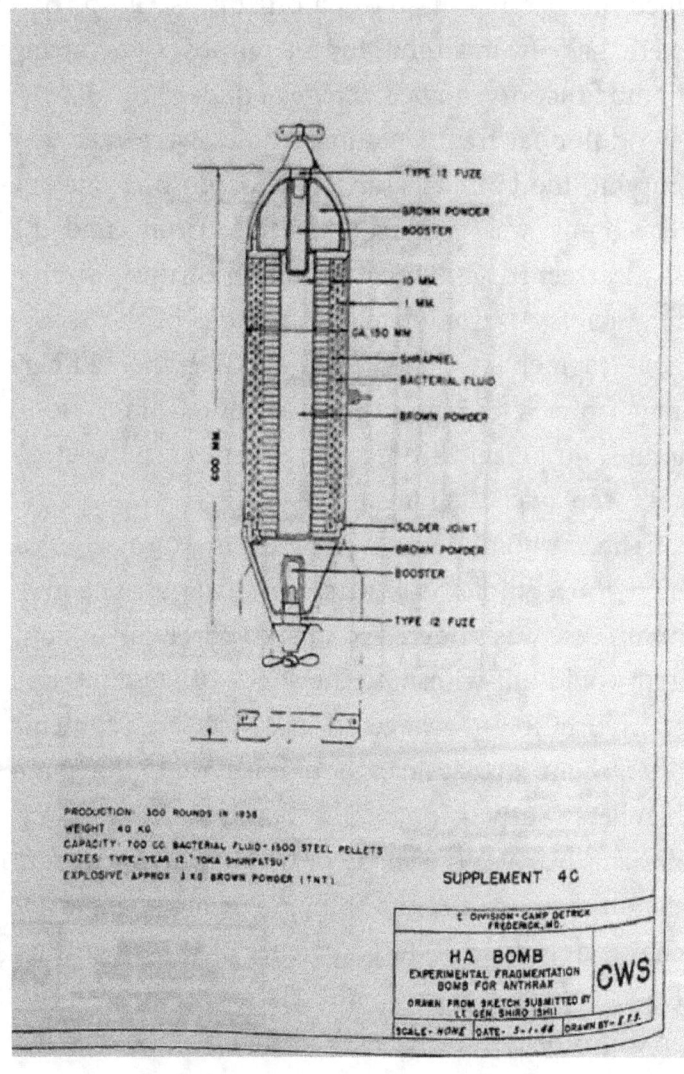

"Ro Bomb—The Ro bomb, in size and appearance, was similar to the I bomb. The head was of novel design containing front and rear compartments. Upon contact with the ground, the front compartment exploded throwing the bomb proper 10 to 15 meters into the air. The rear compartment when exploded, blowing out the tail and ejecting the contents. The bomb fill for the trials was the same as in case of the I bomb, and it was tested on a similar grid. In statis trails an area of dispersion same as with the I bomb. The percentage of duds was greater than in case of the I bomb largely due to the same defective fuzes. For the same reasons as in the case of the I bomb, the Ro bomb was not considered worthy of improvement and was discarded."

Marutas of Unit 731

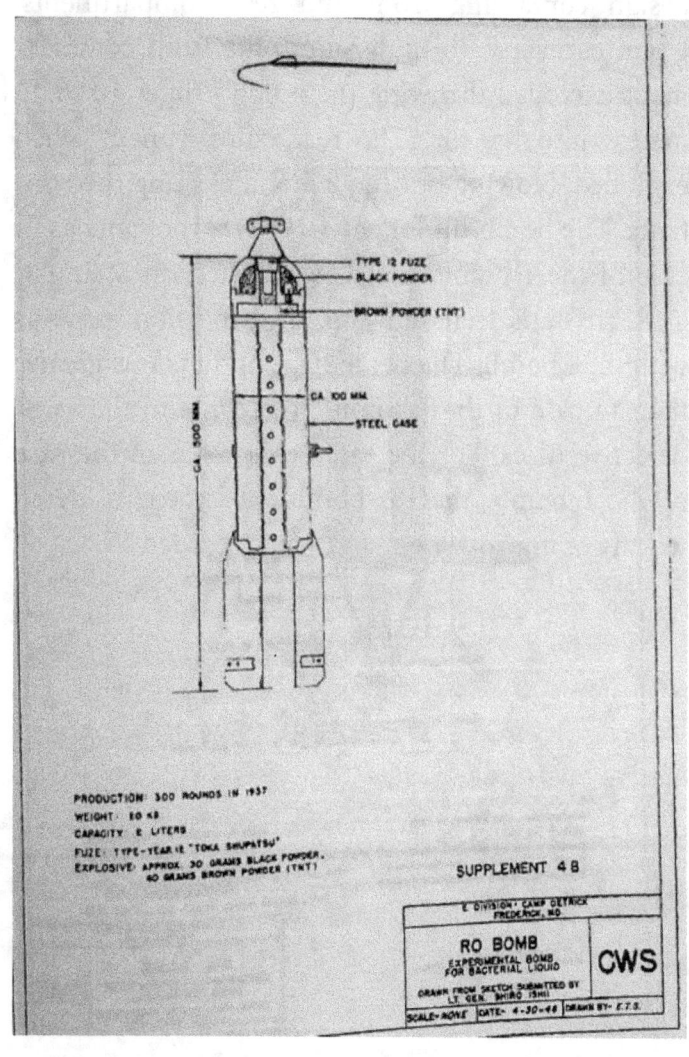

"I Bomb—The I Bomb, a 20kg modified gas bomb with a capacity of 2 liters, was perhaps the first munition developed for the dissemination of a bacterial liquid payload. Explosion of the bomb head upon impact with the ground blew out the tail with ejection of the liquid fill. The bomb was tested during 1937-1938 by static and drop trials from aircraft. For the trials, the bomb was filled to about 70 percent capacity with 0.1 percent fuchain, 2 to 5 percent starch solution, or noninfectious agents. A rectangular grid 100 x 500 meters, with either test papers or Petri dishes, depending upon the fill, placed at 20 meter intervals, was used for assessment of dispersion. In winter, a background of snow was used as a means of evaluating the effective area of dispersion of the bomb contents. With a wind velocity of 5 meters per second, an area of dispersion 10-15 x 100-150 meters resulted in case of static explosion. When dropped from aircraft, the bomb buried itself before exploding, resulting in a deep funnel-shaped crater with little effective dispersion of the contents. Depth of the crater depended on the height of release. Dropped from an altitude of 1,000 meters, a crater 0.5-1 meter in depth resulted; from 2,000 meters a crater 1-1.5 meter in depth resulted; a 4,000-meter drop caused a crater 2.5-3 meters. Because of the tendency to bury itself before detonation, its small capacity and large percentage of duds, the I Bomb was considered unsatisfactory and was discarded."

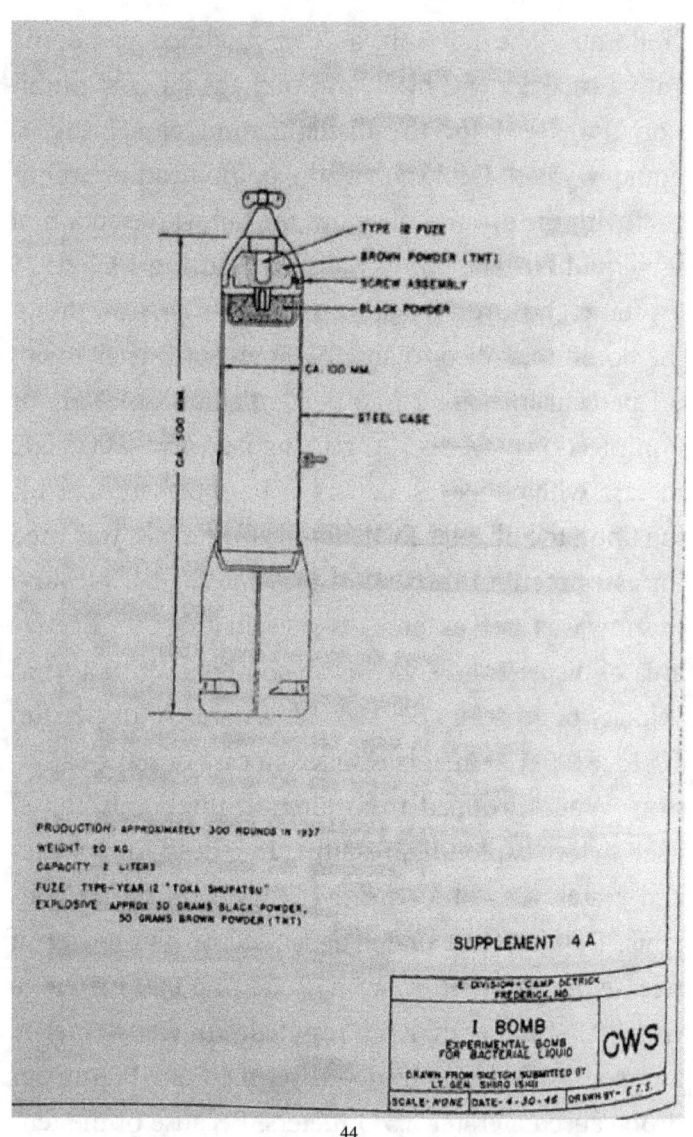

[44] Thompson, Arvo, *Report on Japanese Biological Warfare (BW) Activities*, May 31, 1946

Chapter 7: ANTA Testing Grounds

From November 4, 1944 to March 26, 1945, a total of 69 balloons of Japanese origin were found in the United States, Canada, Alaska, Mexico, and Hawaii. Incendiary bombs were found with eight of the balloons. Fifteen additional incidents of bomb explosions and bomb recoveries have been reported. The balloons were recovered at locations including Washington, Oregon, Kansas, Central California, Northern California, North of Hawaii, Alaska, Nebraska, Wyoming, Montana, and Iowa. The bombs had caused little damage since some were lost at sea, and many fuses did not even detach correctly. However, the Office of Censorship in wartime America issued a message to newspapers and radio stations asking them to remain silent about the balloon incident in order to prevent panic in American public opinion.[45]

---

[45] Col. Alfred McCormack, *War Department Military Intelligence Service, General Report No. 3 on Free Balloons and Related Incidents*, National Archives and Records Administration.

The Sunday Star Pictorial Magazine, June 8, 1947
Washington, D.C.

Paper Weapon

Japanese bomb-carrying balloons designed to terrorize the Western part of the United States were developed until great secrecy and at an estimated cost of $200,000,000 during World War II. Actually used in 1944-45, the weapon caused only a few casualties and slight damage. One balloon landed as far east as Kansas, but had "misplaced" its bomb load somewhere en route. During recent maneuvers, a reconnaissance party of the First Cavalry Division found a number of the launching sites near Otsu, Japan. A sample balloon, inflated for laboratory tests, is a true sphere 100 feet in circumference at its maximum altitude. It is made of five layers of mulberry paper, strong and water repellent when cemented together, and is filled with hydrogen. A device to control altitude is suspended below, and the bomb load with its automatic release mechanism is attached to it. The balloon also is equipped with demolition blocks which are supposed to destroy it in the air, but this attachment failed to operate on several of the balloons which reached this country.

CHAPTER 7: ANTA TESTING GROUNDS

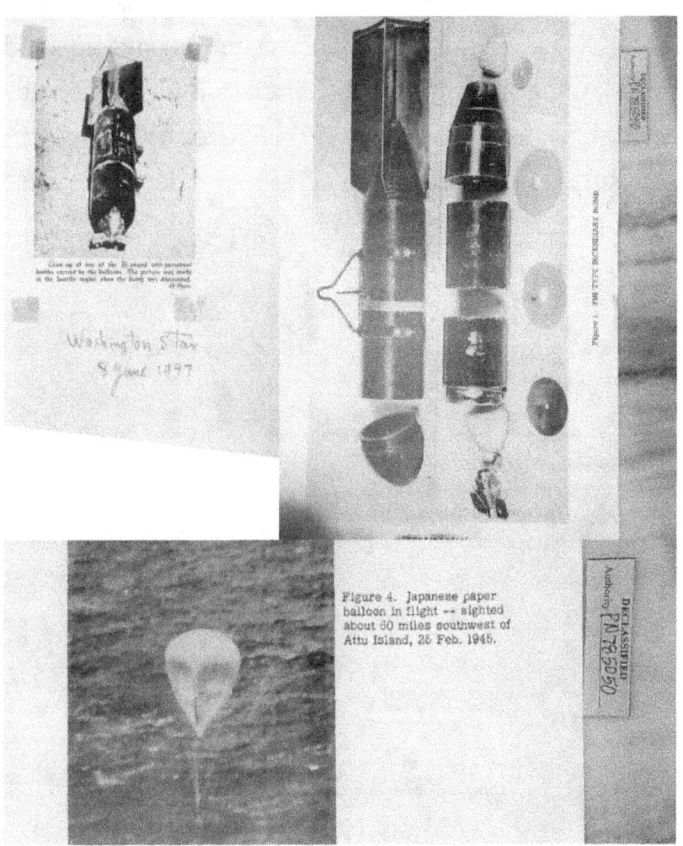

---

[46] *The Sunday Star Pictorial Magazine*, June 8th, 1947.

If the war had not ended in August 1945, Unit 731 would have launched "Cherry Blossom at Night" to spread plague in San Diego at night on September 22, 1945. The operation was a kamikaze mission with Aichi M6A Seiran aircraft carrying plague-infected fleas launched from five I-400 class long-range submarines. The planes were to either drop the plague in balloon bombs or purposely crash in order to disperse the infection to plague the West Coast.[47]

---

[47] LoProto, Mark. "The Secret Japanese Plan for Biological Warfare." *Visit Pearl Harbor*, 13 Oct. 2018.

Chapter 8

Overall Advance from the Laboratory Creations

In the Ishii Network, effectiveness of vaccines was tested on the plentiful supply of prisoners on which to perform tests. Japanese researchers chose a large group of prisoners, vaccinated some of them, infected the whole group with the corresponding diseases, and observed the results, i.e. the death or severe illness of the control group which was not vaccinated. Most of the time with these vaccine testing experiments led to the death of the entire group. Prior to cremation, the bodies underwent pathological and anatomical inspection. The research continued with a new batch of prisoners; researchers strongly believed their strategy reflected proof since results were based on human experimentation rather than theoretical. At the Khabarovsk Trial, witness Furuichi testified about his research experience administering vaccines. As a medical orderly at Branch 643 working in a research group studying pathogenic germs, he later was captured by the Soviet Army on August 17, 1945.

In his recollection, "… at the end of 1943. To test the effectiveness of vaccines, 50 Chinese and Manchurians were used as experimental material. First, these 50 men were given preventive inoculations, but these were differentiated inoculations—some prisoners were given one, others were given two. Furthermore, different men were inoculated with different quantities of vaccine and some of the 50 men were not inoculated at all. Thus the men were divided into five different groups. All of them were forced to drink water contaminated with typhoid germs and were then observed to see what effect these pathogenic germs had in the different cases, depending on whether preventive inoculations had been performed or not, how many times, and in what quantities. Most of these men contracted typhoid. Exactly what percentage I do not remember; at all events 12 or 13 of the men died."[48]

Dr. Futagi Hideo who experimented with BCG on Manchurian children, testing dosages and protection, concluded that with CI Tuberculosis hominis, "all doses produced military tuberculosis which

---

[48] *Khabarovsk Trial*, p. 284

was fatal within one month in those injected with 10.0 and 1.0 mg. The others were severely ill, lived longer, but probably died later."[49]

Other scientists did research on songo fever, typhus, glanders, botulism, brucellosis, gas gangrene, influenza, meningococcus, plague, smallpox, tetanus, tick encephalitis, and tularemia.

These studies enabled the Japanese army to better prepare their soldiers for the battlefield. In an Interrogation Report No. 52 prepared by the Joint Intelligence Center Pacific Ocean Areas on June 6, 1944, Ken Kato revealed the types of vaccines the Japanese Army administered. His troop was given immunization against typhoid, paratyphoid A, paratyphoid B, bacillary dysentery, botulinus, and cholera. Gas gangrene and tetanus prophylaxis immunization were administered to the wounded. Salmonella immunization also was administered. The vaccines were produced at the Army Medical School in the Ushigome section of Tokyo.[50]

At the end of the war, the allies occupied the Empire of Japan and compiled a list of Japanese drugs and medicines at the direction of the Chief Surgeon.

---

[49] Technical Library, Fort Dugway Proving Grounds, Utah, Tuberculosis, Interview with Dr. Hideo Gutagi on November 15th, 1947

[50] *Joint intelligence Center Pacific Ocean Areas Interrogation Report No. 52.*

This was to reduce the Allied force's cost of shipping medicine to occupied Japan. The list included water purification tablets, malaria medicine, mosquito repellent, water chlorination kits, antistreptococcal serum, vaccines for gas gangrene, dysentery, and typhoid, typhoid serum, athlete's foot medication, and others to show that the Ishii Network had been very productive and interconnected with Japanese corporations.

The ties that Unit 731 had with medical fields in Japanese universities sped the process by which pharmaceutical companies could produce based on research. University researchers who were considered civilian employees and conducted independent research in Unit 731 had ties to Tokyo and Kyoto University. They were also on a rotation program for their research as visiting scholars. One could be sure that they returned home with their results and were ready to excel at a job interview with a private employer to heighten the productivity of pharmaceutical companies in Japan.[51]

---

[51] Gold, Hal, *Unit 731 Testimony*, p. 60

CHAPTER 8: OVERALL ADVANCE FROM THE LABORATORY CREATIONS

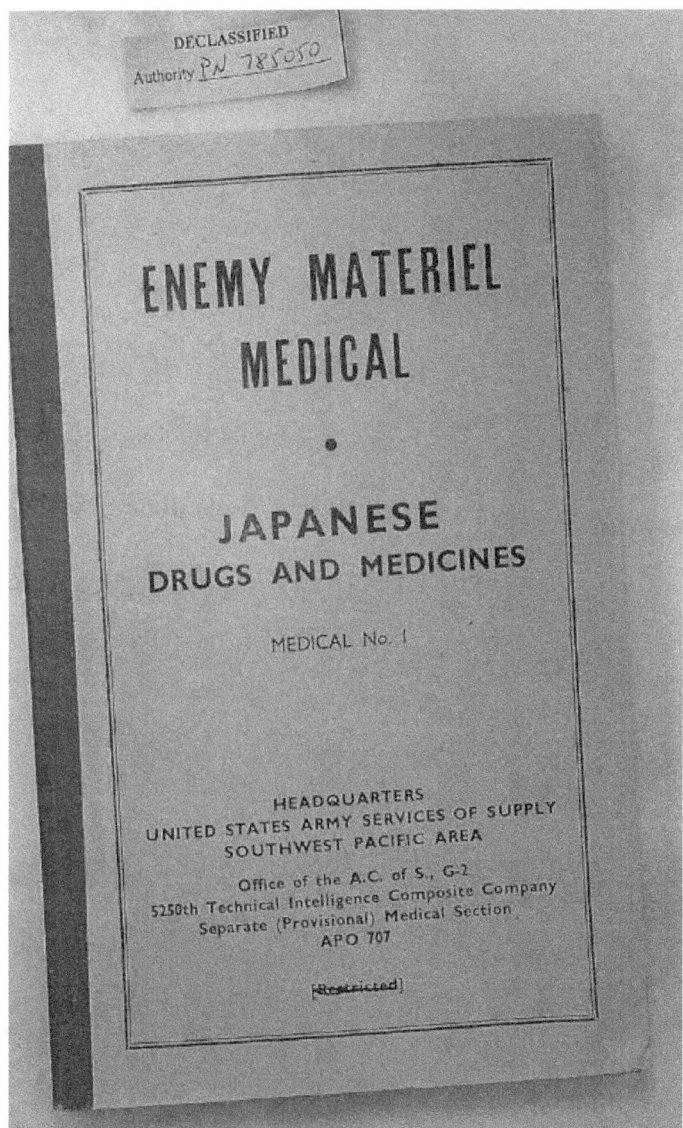

Chapter 9

The End of the War

The surrender of the puppet emperor of Manchuria, Henry Puyi on August 16, 1945.

No one in Unit 731 saw the end of the war coming in August of 1945. The Soviets had formally declared war on Imperial Japan and had launched an attack into Northeast China and Korea. Due to the rapid progression of Soviet Union troops, Unit 731 was unable to continue their operation. On August 9th, General Yamada, the Commander in Chief of the Kwantung Army, signed an order to destroy Unit 731.[52] The buildings were dynamited and all prisoners were cremated and cast into the Songhuajiang River outside of Harbin.[53]

According to one of the nurses, Akama Masako, in the final days of Unit 731, she was, "… with the syphilitic mothers; the doctor in charge of our team delivered the maruta babies himself instead of having the nurses do it, as would normally be the case. At that time, he would order me to stop the blood flow from the mother to the baby. The doctor would take a sample of the blood, then I would let small quantities of blood flow intermittently, as he took successive samples. The test tubes were all lined up on the shelf. He was checking to determine the intensity of the syphilis transmitted from mother to child and the progression of the disease from the time of birth. A researcher came running in, screaming that some maruta had escaped. They were caught by the Special Forces, the team under Ishii Shiro's brother, Ishii Takeo. Only someone who could be trusted was admitted to that team. They shot the escapees.

---

[52] *Khabarovsk Trial*, p. 271.
[53] Tsuchiya, Takashi, *Japanese Medical Atrocities 1932-1945: What, Who, How, and Why?*, p. 5, 2005.

Chapter 9: The End of the War

When it came time to evacuate, we got into a train and left the unit headquarters. It was a long train, maybe twenty or thirty cars. A soldier came running to me and said that a baby was going to be born in a freight car at the end of the train. We ran back through the cars. The wife of one of the unit members was there in labor, and there were soldiers with lots of medals. Surrounded by those high-ranking officers, I delivered the baby. That was August 15, 1945. We were passing through Xinjing. The train engineer ran away and we could not move. Planes were flying overhead, keeping lookout; soldiers were around us. I was trembling in fear. This, I felt, was really war. Then, we heard the emperor's words ending the war. We were always told to "work hard and Japan will definitely win." When I heard that we had lost, I was sad. It grew dark. Ishii came over to us carrying a big candle and said, 'I'm sending you all back home. When you get there, if any one of you gives away the secret of Unit 731, I personally will find you, even if I have to part the roots of the grass to do it.' He had a fearful diabolical look on his face—my legs were shaking—and not just at me—at everyone. 'Even if I have to part the grasses…'"[54]

---

[54] Gold, Hal, *Unit 731 Testimony*, p. 128.

After escaping, Ishii faked his death, but was found by the CIA.[55] When they learned that Ishii possessed valuable information they did not want falling into Soviet hands as the Cold War was about to start, the CIA worked with Ishii to keep the Soviet Union from bringing him to justice at the Khabarovsk Trial. Out of the 3607 members of Unit 731, only 12 were brought to Soviet Union for the Khabarovsk Trial and most were released by 1956 except for one who committed suicide in a Soviet jail. The west often dismissed the Khabarovsk Trial as communist propaganda, but it was one of the more revealing interrogations of Unit 731. The other scientists traded their research results from Unit 731 for immunity from the United States. The U.S.'s Camp Detrick was the recipient of that information. Most scientists who worked at Unit 731 ended up with promising careers in Japanese politics or the pharmaceutical industry. In 1959, Ishii died peacefully from laryngeal cancer.

---

[55] Report of November 10th, 1945 on Ishii's staged funeral in Chiba, National Archives and Records Administration, RG 290, Box 12.

OTHER RELATED BOOKS

www.ingramcontent.com/pod-product-compliance
Lightning Source LLC
Chambersburg PA
CBHW050327120526
44592CB00014B/2076